Karl Julius Schröer
and Rudolf Steiner

Karl Julius Schröer and Rudolf Steiner

Anthroposophy and the Teachings of Karma and Reincarnation

LUIGI MORELLI

iUniverse books may be ordered through booksellers or by contacting:

iUniverse
1663 Liberty Drive
Bloomington, IN 47403
www.iuniverse.com
1-800-Authors (1-800-288-4677)

ISBN: 978-1-4917-7126-6 (sc)

Print information available on the last page.

iUniverse rev. date: 10/17/2016

CONTENTS

INTRODUCTION

This work had been in progress for seven or eight years when the book *Rudolf Steiner's Core Mission,* by Thomas H. Meyer, came out in an English edition in 2010; that book came into my hands just before Christmas of that year. Consequently, my focus changed, so that the reader may find less repetition here, and more new information, to complement what is found in *Rudolf Steiner's Core Mission.* Meyer's book brings to light the depth of the assertion that Steiner's task was the spreading of a spiritual-scientific understanding of karma and reincarnation. It is true that this thought has been repeated with frequency in various anthroposophical circles over the years, but no written work has taken on the specific task of exploring in depth the matter of this particular issue. I give credit to Meyer for addressing a long-needed assessment of Steiner's core life task in a more comprehensive way than had been done heretofore. This work expands Meyer's perspective by deepening the exploration of the differences between what would have been Karl Julius Schröer's and Steiner's contributions to spiritual-scientific understanding and practice in the twentieth century.

If, as I have heard expressed in frequent conversations, Schröer's task was to bring humanity the gift of anthroposophy; and if Steiner was meant to restore the teachings of karma and reincarnation in a Christianized way; then certainly Steiner's task would be as large a task as Schröer's more familiar one has been. It certainly does not help that, at present, the boundaries between one and the other task are blurred, both from a historical perspective and from a practical one. Nevertheless, when we say Steiner was meant to bring the teachings of karma and reincarnation, we are only at the beginning of a whole series of new questions. How do those teachings stand in relation to what was intended as the foundations of anthroposophy? What are the depth, breadth, and uniqueness of this impulse? What are its manifestations and applications? Moreover, we should not expect that Steiner's mission was simply of the same nature as what should have preceded it in Schröer's task, a simple addition in an interrupted continuum.

In what ways does the impulse meant to be Steiner's differ from that of Schröer's? Certainly, two initiates bring not only different teachings, but also teachings that are differentiated in their modality, scope, and aims. So, it is legitimate to ask oneself how the two world missions— Steiner's and Schröer's—stand in relation to each other. And by this question, I mean, "How do they complement one another? Where do they address different faculties in the human being?" A parallel would clarify this question. When philosophy moved from Plato's worldview to Aristotle's, new requirements were put before the human being. A pupil could not simply move from being a follower of Plato to studying Aristotle unless he had been willing to face a discontinuity; that is, he had to be willing to undergo a rigorous training of his thinking by means of Aristotle's logic. Plato made no such exacting demand upon his students.

Questions also arise at another level. The disruption of karma caused by Schröer's falling short of his world task certainly had more than one consequence for humanity. One consequence that we can intuit is that Steiner could not bring his own impulse to full fruition. In fact, by Steiner's own admission, we know that his life task was fully resumed only after the Christmas Foundation Meeting at the end of 1923. Shortly after that world turning-point, with Steiner's death in March, 1925, the Anthroposophical Society was tragically denied the guidance and inspiration of the one who had re-founded it. So we could ask ourselves, how has the karma of the Michaelic Movement been affected ever since?

The latter question brings up a very closely related question. What is the present karma of Platonists and Aristotelians? What are the consequences in relation to the idea of culmination that Steiner placed at the center of the renewal of culture in pour times? This book is already approaching the question indirectly, since we will be talking of the destiny of the eternal souls of Plato/Schröer and Aristotle/Steiner.

However, discussing this would burden the presentation, so I have decided to present it separately.

Steiner left numerous traces in his many lectures, clues about the callings of his karma, and how world karma had to be adjusted and modified in order to compensate for disturbances in its own unfolding. The dedicated work of researchers over decades has uncovered many of these traces. Some of the indications that allow us to rebuild the currents at work in the most important story of the twentieth century, lie hidden in plain view. Others have been found through combing the correspondence and memoirs of all those in whom Steiner confided. They have come to light gradually over many decades so that at present, they are available even to those who, like the author, do not have access to the original German documents.

This book is built around three main sources. One cardinal document is formed by the whole lecture cycle known as *Karmic Relationships*, Volume 4, which I have dubbed "Steiner's spiritual testament." A second source is the *Autobiography*. To these sources, we add many other threads of research and general considerations that add substance to, and render more explicit, what the previous material offers to our understanding.

The first chapter dwells on the content of *Karmic Relationships*, Volume 4, which could be considered Steiner's spiritual testament. Three related themes throw light on Steiner's mission and on world karma. The first is Steiner's revelation about the importance of the teachings of karma and reincarnation in the history of the Theosophical and Anthroposophical Societies. A theme that occupies center stage is Steiner's relationship to the Cistercians. The lecture cycle closes in a climax with the revelation of Schröer's life task. Each thread on its own forms a riddle, but if we see the threads woven together, an answer starts to emerge.

The heart of this book, in the second, third and fourth chapters, explores what lay at the center of Steiner's own life task, in its full implications. The theme is first approached from a historical standpoint in Chapter 2, and followed from the perspective of modern anthroposophical trends in the next chapter. It is completed in Chapter 4 with an outline of the path of Spirit Recollection, which is the term that best embraces the inner practices associated with the realities of karma and reincarnation.

Chapter 5 explores the two main tasks that Steiner carried to completion. It contrasts those paths that in the Foundation Stone Meditation are called Spirit Recollection or Spirit Remembering (first panel) and Spirit Vision or Spirit Beholding (third panel). It is only natural to follow this contrast by rounding off the picture with the middle term of the Foundation Stone Meditation: the practice of Spirit Mindfulness or Spirit Awareness (panel 2). This is only a very short exploration, since it does not touch on the heart of this book's investigation.

The last chapter explores the breadth of the applications deriving from the teachings of karma and reincarnation. It places these in relation to the seven life processes described by Steiner, and opens up the vista on the further development of the teachings of karma and reincarnation and their practical applications.

CHAPTER 1

KARL JULIUS SCHRÖER'S AND RUDOLF STEINER'S MISSIONS

There is a natural progression from *Karmic Relationships*, Volume 3 to Volume 4. We could say that Volume 3 is about the past of the Michaelic movement. Volume 4 touches on only one portion of that history, the part that pertains to the destiny relationship between Karl Julius Schröer and Rudolf Steiner. In addition, Volume 4 looks at Steiner's path of destiny in relation to world karma. It is the portion of world karma that colors the present and the immediate future. It is no wonder that Steiner completed his *Autobiography*, delivered the lectures of *Karmic Relationships*, Volume 4, and barely managed to speak about Saint John in his *Last Address*, through which he was offering us insights about individualities who will play a role in the future. All along, he must have felt a sense of urgency for anthroposophists to know what was at stake. The 1922 "Hague Conversation" with Walter Johannes Stein follows these themes, amplifies some, and allows us to build further threads. To this one I will return in the following volume. Let us look at the chronology of all these revelations:

-   1922, The Hague: Steiner spoke to Stein, entrusting him with important revelations about his own karma and world karma.

-   End of 1923–1924, Dornach: Christmas Foundation Meeting.

-   July 1–13, 1924, Dornach: six lectures, now in *Karmic Relationships*, Volume 3, *Karma of the Michaelic Movement.*

-   July 18–20, Arnhem: three lectures in Arnhem, now in *Karmic Relationships*, Volume 6. All these lectures deal with the karma of the Michaelic Movement; in fact a continuation or recapitulation of Volume 3.

-   July 28–August 8, Dornach: five lectures, now in Volume 3, *Karma of the Michaelic Movement.*

-   August 12–August 27, Torquay and London: six lectures now in *Karmic Relationships*, Volume 8; mostly touching on the karma of the Michaelic Movement, and introducing the Arthur and the Grail streams and their mutual relationships.

-   September 5–23, Dornach: ten lectures now gathered in *Karmic Relationships*, Volume 4.

-   September 24, Dornach: lecture "How Did Man Originate? Earth Life and Star Wisdom." Only lecture given between *Karmic Relationships*, Volume 4, and the *Last Address.*

-   September 28, 1924, Dornach: *Last Address.*

-   December 1923 to April 1925: *Autobiography.*

We will now look at two closely interrelated themes and their consequences both for Steiner and for the karma of the Anthroposophical Society. In *Karmic Relationships,* Volume 4, Steiner explained in some depth his relationship with Karl Julius Schröer on the one hand. On the other hand, he returned a few times, and with equal emphasis, to his relationship with the Cistercians in his childhood and early youth, and with the circle around Maria Eugenia delle Grazie in the Vienna years. The two broad themes, although intimately interrelated, are not explicitly linked. The structure of the lectures and the themes treated bring them to intertwine; one riddle is the answer to the other. With the help of other sources, we can see how in the two themes another larger theme weaves in, which we can call "world karma." To this we turn our attention at present, starting by familiarizing ourselves with the figure of Karl Julius Schröer.

Karl Julius Schröer and Goethe

Scarcely any other figure could play as important a part in Aristotle/ Steiner's life than the reincarnated Plato/ Schröer. We will now follow the evolution of the soul who played an important part in forming much of the Western worldview, Plato; and of Goethe, who had been a follower of Platonism in a previous incarnation.

Plato descended from one of the oldest families in Athens, and claimed ancestry from Solon, the lawgiver and poet. Socrates, who had been his teacher, died when Plato reached age twenty-one. Before that Plato had been a dramatist, orator, actor, and poet. The death of his teacher, Socrates, prompted his decision to write down the *Dialogues*, in order to glorify the method of Socrates' dialectic; and it set the stage for the rise of Plato the philosopher and orator. Soon after, the young philosopher went to Megara, associating himself with Euclid. Then he traveled to Egypt, Cyrene, Magna Grecia, and Sicily, returning to Athens at about age forty.

The ideas present in Plato's *Dialogues* had their origin in the mission of Dionysus. The *Dialogues* inaugurated the method of thinking, just as the Dionysian Mysteries previously led to clairvoyance.[1] The Platonic *Dialogues* were dramas of knowledge, leading to a *catharsis* in which the Dionysian principle now lived as a force of conscience, appearing as the voice of the *daimon*. Plato looked back to the past of the world's existence; at the personal level this culminated in the *anamnesis*, the soul's remembrance of existence before its birth in the world of ideas.

Plato's worldview lived in the conundrum that objects can be seen but not thought, and ideas can be thought but not seen, that led

---

[1] Frederick Hiebel, *The Gospel of Hellas: the Mission of Ancient Greece and the Advent of Christ.*

ultimately to the dichotomy of matter and spirit. This dichotomy was further expressed in the idea that the body was the prison of the spirit. On the other hand, the last inklings and memories of reincarnation survived in Plato, together with the idea of the pre-existence of the soul. These are expressed in his *Meno, Phaedrus,* and in the *Republic.*

Platonism survived through the Middle Ages, most significantly of all in what was called the School of Chartres. However, it was difficult for Plato to look down at what survived on earth as Platonism. According to Steiner's research in *Karmic Relationships* Volume 4: "…it was for him only too frequently a dreadful disturbance in his supersensible life of soul and spirit."[2] He had great difficulty returning to earth; and, entering the Christian epoch, to find a body in which he might carry his former soul inclinations. This was because Plato had been a Greek, steeped in the artistic element. The subsequent civilization had acquired the Roman stamp through and through; and neo-Platonism lived on only in a pale copy of what Platonism had been. All of this explains the difficulty for Plato's soul in seeking re-embodiment. We also hear in the same lecture, "And there was also a certain difficulty for his nature to receive Christianity; for he himself represented in a certain sense the highest point of the pre-Christian conception of the world."[3]

Plato reincarnated as the tenth century nun Hroswitha, who belonged to the convent of Gandersheim in Brunswick (Lower Saxony, Germany). Already at that time, she united strongly with the mid-European-Germanic spirit. However, she was reticent in receiving and working through the Roman coloring of the culture. This may have been a further cause for delay in her soul.

Little is known about Hroswitha's origin and life. The fact that she had been accepted at the royal abbey of Gandersheim implies that she was of a noble family. Under the reign of King Otto I (936–973), the abbey had been awarded autonomous power; it responded only to the control of provosts appointed by the king, not to any other secular or religious authority. The women living at Gandersheim agreed to regulate their

---

[2] Steiner, *Karmic Relationships*, Volume 4, September 23, 1923 lecture.
[3] Steiner, *Karmic Relationships*, Volume 4, September 23, 1923 lecture.

conduct by a rule, but did not take permanent vows. As a result, people moved freely between court and abbey, promoting a lively exchange of ideas. Otto (Emperor of Germany, Austria, Switzerland, and Northern Italy) had promoted a little renaissance at his court. Writers and artists came to see him from all over Europe, and Hroswitha enjoyed access to much of the written material of her time.

Hroswitha wrote from about 960 to shortly after 973. At the end of this period, she apparently organized her writing into three books in what was likely a chronological sequence. Book 1, *Historia,* mostly contains five legends; Book 2 centers around six dramas; in Book 3 are found two epic poems: *Gesta Ottonis* (The Deeds of King Otto), and a narrative of the beginnings of the Abbey of Gandersheim. Nothing is known of Hroswitha's later life.

Hroswitha's dramas are narrated in a dialogue form that harkens back to Plato. Even though she portrayed dramatic stories, they were not written for the stage. The striving that runs through them could be expressed in terms of the question of how to Christianize art. This is what she did under the influence of the Roman dramatist Terence, whom she took as a model. She did not write comedies like as he did; rather, she used her stories as a means to educate the soul. Interestingly, she was also the first writer to introduce the theme of Faust, in her *Theophilus.* He, too, is a soul that ever struggles forward, and because of this he can find redemption even after each fall.

Although Hroswitha von Gandersheim had a certain influence upon her time, this incarnation was a considerable step down from what one would expect from the reincarnated Plato. One would easily expect that he would have incarnated among the teachers of the School of Chartres. In effect, neo-Platonism received its major impulses without a fundamental contribution from its primary protagonist. This element seems to explain the soul's later difficulties.

After this time the soul partook of the transition of the Platonic stream into the spiritual world. Hroswitha returned to earth as Karl Julius Schröer. In his youth, he intuited how middle Middle Europe could not live in the Roman element, and saw it in his mind's eye as a modern Greece. Schröer's earlier feminine nature recoiled from the strong masculine tenor of the time's intellectualism; and he suffered greatly from being misunderstood. People would either take sides with him, or disparage him. Many would in fact assert that praising Schröer was a sign of poor judgment.

Plato had cultivated a very affectionate relationship toward a Greek artist who later reincarnated as Goethe. The Greek incarnation of Goethe lived under Plato's influence, although not as a pupil. He could be called a follower in the artistic realm. Steiner characterizes their relationship as "noble and pure." The philosopher Plato could perceive how much lay in his friend's soul that was of promise to the future of humanity.

In the life between death and rebirth the incarnating Goethe absorbed from the Jupiter sphere the transformed essence of what he had taken from Platonic philosophy. He evolved it further, and it permeated everything that he undertook in his earthly life. The strong tie between Goethe's soul and Plato manifested in Schröer's incarnation with a desire to show humanity the importance of Goethe's work.

Schröer's Relationship to Anthroposophy

Steiner's relationship with Schröer was colored from the beginning with great affection. In *The Riddle of Man* (1916), Steiner describes Schröer's personality and achievements. Nevertheless, in Steiner's biography, the difficulties or puzzles he had with this great thinker appear here and there quite clearly.

When still in college, Steiner started experimenting in order to refute Newton's thinking. He had already written some papers about his results and shown them to Schröer, who had shown little interest. Steiner later found out that Goethe had conducted similar experiments. He then repeated all the experiments of Goethe, and showed them to Schröer, who finally showed his utmost interest. In conclusion, Steiner commented, "It pleased Schröer tremendously when I expressed such views, but he never went beyond that." And, referring to another instance, Steiner concluded, "Once again, I felt entirely alone in my struggle with this enigma [the scientific Goethe]."[4] Even so, Steiner continued to read

---

[4] Steiner, *Autobiography*, Chapter 15.

Goethe with new excitement. He often reread the conversation between Schiller and Goethe about the *Urpflanze* (archetypal plant), deriving much solace from it at times when he felt very isolated at the core of his being.

Steiner described how pleased Schröer was when others could acknowledge the validity of Goethe's scientific work. When a colleague had emphasized that Newton had opposed Goethe, and that Newton was a genius, Schröer added to Steiner, "But Goethe was also a genius."[5] Goethe had such an influence on Schröer's life that Steiner could say of this particular relationship, "Whenever I was alone with Schröer in this way, I always felt that yet a third was present—the spirit of Goethe. Schröer lived so strongly in Goethe's being and works, that with every thought and feeling that arose in him he asked himself, 'Would Goethe have felt and thought in this way?'"[6] Schröer was already editing *Faust* for the Kürschner publishing house; he could have gone on to edit the scientific work as well. However, at this point, he proposed that Kürschner should appoint Steiner for the task. Kürschner took the risk, solely on the recommendation of Schröer, since Steiner was virtually unknown. Schröer perfectly understood that the height of Goethe's scientific studies had remained unequaled. Steiner concluded: "Schröer saw a descent from Goethe's spiritual height in the worldview of the scientific age that followed him. Schröer's foreword [to the edition of *German National Literature*] comprehensively characterized my assigned task in editing Goethe's writings on science."[7]

Schröer felt that Goethe's scientific research was the work of a genius, but his withdrawal from intellectuality left Steiner alone to deal with the matter. Steiner had noticed that his friend's ideas arose from a certain level of intuition, but that otherwise, he had no interest in structuring his world of thoughts.[8] "Had he attained intellectuality, had he been able to unite it with the spirituality of Plato, anthroposophy itself would have been there," is Steiner's revealing conclusion in the last lecture in *Karmic*

---

[5] Steiner, *Autobiography*, Chapter 15.
[6] Steiner, *Karmic Relationships*, Volume 4, September 23, 1923 lecture.
[7] Steiner, *Autobiography*, Chapter 7.
[8] Ibid, Chapter 9.

Relationships, Volume 4. He added in his *Autobiography*, "Anthroposophy would really have been his [Schröer's] calling.… The very thing which he bears within him from a former incarnation, if it could enter into the intellect, would have become Anthroposophy; it stops short; it recoils, as it were, from intellectualism."[9]

Steiner recalled that early in his relationship with Schröer, he had expressed an element of opposition to his teacher. In an example from his days at the Vienna Technical College, Steiner mentioned once writing an essay on Mephisto, motivated primarily by a desire to oppose his teacher.[10] At another point, Schröer was displeased with Steiner's use of Johann Friedrich Herbart's philosophy to explore the question, "To what extent is a human being free in terms of actions?"[11] Another bone of contention was Schröer's inability to raise himself beyond partisan concerns. Thus he could not understand Steiner's views on education, which Steiner shared in "The German Weekly," and through which he exclusively took the stance of what promoted cultural evolution, moving beyond political and nationalistic concerns to which Schröer subscribed.[12] The above examples illustrate how Schröer refused to discipline his thinking. For this reason, among others, Schröer never felt fully at home in his body, and later contracted a condition that Steiner called "feeble-mindedness." Schröer's inability to move beyond his entrenched sympathies and antipathies could have been corrected by the development of his intellect, followed by the transcendence of intellectualism; but Schröer stopped short of those tasks.

After speaking of how Schröer shrank from his task, Steiner

---

[9] Steiner, *Karmic Relationships*, Volume 4, September 23, 1923 lecture.
[10] Steiner and Schröer's reacted differently to the reading of "Robespierre," M. E. delle Grazie's pessimistic poem. "Schröer was indignant. In his view, art should not delve into such a 'bottomless abyss of horror.'" Disagreeing with him, Steiner wrote the article "Nature and Our Ideals," basically appraising realistic pessimism over shallow optimism that closes itself to the abysses of existence. Schröer, taking this in a deeply personal way, was unable to understand his friend. Ironically, he was the one who had spoken very highly of delle Grazie's earlier work. (Steiner, *Autobiography*, Chapter 18).
[11] Steiner, *Autobiography*, Chapter 9.
[12] Ibid, Chapter 22.

continued, "But as I said, what else could one do, than loose the congestion that had taken place, and carry Goetheanism really onward into Anthroposophy." And he concluded, "I resolved at that time to live Schröer's destiny as my own, and relinquish my own path of destiny."[13] In the published version of their conversation, Stein wrote that Rudolf Steiner could return to his mission only through the Christmas Conference of 1923; "whereas everything that lay between was taken over from the path which Schröer should have trodden." This was made more explicit in reply to Stein's question about what part of Schröer's task Steiner had taken over. "The whole teaching of Imagination, Inspiration, and Intuition, and everything up to the forms of the Goetheanum building," was the answer.[14]

Plato had very much brought the end of Mystery teaching, ushering in the conditions for modern humanity before Christ's appearance at the turning point of time. However, with Plato's teaching, matter stood divorced from spirit in an untenable dichotomy. Much of Western thought suffered in the following centuries from what Steiner characterized as the resulting "one-sidedness of Platonism." Steiner was uniquely fitted to undertake and further the task that Schröer could not fully assume. Steiner's efforts led to the elaboration of spiritual/scientific methodology and knowledge. Two of his previous incarnations, in particular, had created the foundations for such an elaboration of knowledge. Aristotle had completed the divorce of knowledge from its ancient original sources in the Mysteries. He did that without betraying the nature of its sources in the spirit; rather, he adapted knowledge to the emerging consciousness bound to thinking. Thomas Aquinas (Steiner's subsequent incarnation) continued this necessary trend; he had to acknowledge the limits of thinking, leading to the differentiation between science and faith. In so doing, he safeguarded the possibility of leading knowledge beyond the dead ends that Arabism and Nominalism

---

[13] Steiner, *Karmic Relationships*, Volume 4, September 23, 1923 lecture.

[14] *Twin Roads to the Millennium*, Hans Peter von Manen, 170. Original quote from *Korrespondenz der Anthroposophischen Arbeitsgemeinschaft*, Volume III, No 5, February 1934.

presented to humanity. Steiner led this cycle to its completion, by laying out the basis for modern spiritual scientific knowledge. He did this at a time when humanity could take a new step toward understanding of the spiritual world.

One can assume that taking on the whole of Schröer's task meant an inner sacrifice for Steiner, as he himself mentioned, particularly in the last of his lectures in the *Karmic Relationships* cycles. Some of that inner tension also can be seen in his *Autobiography*:

> Looking back, I realize that I owe much to the struggle for the development of my spiritual experiences of cognition. Because my destiny brought me the Goethe task as part of my life, this development was slowed considerably. Otherwise, I would have pursued my spiritual experiences, and described them exactly as they presented themselves to me. My consciousness would have widened into the spiritual world more rapidly, but I would have felt no need to work hard at penetrating my inner being.[15]

Steiner's core mission, that of spreading the Christianized teachings of karma and reincarnation, was done under the most trying of circumstances, and because of those, it was undoubtedly slowed and delayed. We can rightfully ask ourselves how both impulses that Steiner promoted (Schröer's and his own) have evolved since the days of the Christmas Conference, and what is the resulting world karma.

What has emerged from looking at Schröer's eternal biography, will acquire further clarity when complemented with what Steiner revealed about the "disturbances" suffered in his own karma.

Steiner's Spiritual Testament

Let us find our way more deeply into the matter of Steiner's task, looking at his own words. There is an important document that may be

---

[15] Steiner, *Autobiography,* Chapter 27.

considered Steiner's "spiritual testament"—the cycle of lectures known as *Karmic Relationships*, Volume 4.

Karmic Relationships, Volume 4 is the last cycle of lectures that Steiner ever gave. Throughout the lectures, he disclosed biographical information much more intimate than any he had given before. These revelations form a complement to his biography, and throw much light upon his life task. In fact, the whole cycle of lectures was given in such a way that it can help us to understand Steiner's life mission in relation to the incarnations of other highly evolved individuals and initiates in the time of the Consciousness Soul. These revelations throw light upon world karma, and follow on the premises of the karma of the Michael streams of Aristotelians and Platonists, in *Karmic Relationships,* Volume 3.

The lectures of the third Volume outline the historic occult background, which creates the prelude to the spiritual/cultural battles of the present— what B. J. Lievegoed calls the "battle for the soul." Within this battle, the Michaelic streams of humanity play their role at the side of Christ. These streams were prepared first in the School of Chartres and in Scholasticism, and ever since the beginning of the Fifth Post-Atlantean Age, through participation in the heavenly Michael School, which culminated in the supersensible *cultus* at the turn of the eighteenth and nineteenth centuries. Biographically, Steiner spoke of a battle in which his individuality was always present and played a determining role. In his last incarnation before the present, Steiner/Aquinas had played an important role in Christianizing thought, and in wresting it from tendencies that either tied thought to the past (by holding back individuality, as in Arabism), or went too far ahead of their time (by divorcing the human being from soul and spirit, as in Nominalism). This is the battle that Steiner continued in the present with the inauguration of the modern Mysteries.

Volume 4 continues where Volume 3 left off. It takes us to the scene of the modern incarnations, and it shows us what Steiner's soul struggled with in its last incarnation. But there is yet another dimension. Although Volume 3 could be defined as "world karma as it was meant to be," Volume 4 is much more subtle and contextualized. Volume 4 introduces us to the world of alternative scenarios; the world that is the reality of the Age of the Consciousness Soul; the time in which conquering and transforming intellectualism represents a mighty cosmic test. Now more than ever, there are no predetermined outcomes for the human race, and every individual contribution plays a part that alters the earthly/cosmic pattern.

Let us summarize the lectures in question. What strikes the reader is the frankness with which Steiner spoke of many intimate aspects of his biography. Anthroposophists are accustomed to Steiner's habitual reticence; his self-references are extremely rare and almost always prefaced with apologies. In this instance he was disclosing something far from personal; in fact, these disclosures revealed world karma.

Significantly, the cycle began with indirect indications about Steiner's life task, and returned to the same theme at the end, in relation to Schröer's biography and mission. Lecture 1 of the cycle starts by telling us about Steiner's intentions in regard to the teaching of karma and reincarnation, and how that mission was delayed for twenty-two years. In Lecture 2, Steiner looked at the karmic biographies of Ludwig Schleich and August Strindberg. The central theme is that of two souls, whose development evolves in diverging directions, according to the morality of their choices.

Lecture 3 delves into the karma of the Michaelites, as exemplified most clearly in Aristotle and Alexander, and in the opposing forces working through Haroun al Raschid and Amos Comenius. Here, Steiner was talking about his and Ita Wegman's eternal individualities in one of their Greek incarnations. In Lecture 4, Steiner went with more depth into the working of the School of Michael, and into the roles of Platonists in the School of Chartres, and of Aristotelians in Scholasticism. He then introduced the figure of Julian the Apostate, from various angles. First, Steiner gave an assessment of Julian's life and mission, through which it appears that Julian was one of the most important figures of early Christianity. Julian could have achieved the task of reconciling the knowledge of the pagan Sun Mysteries with the historical figure of Jesus Christ. In that regard he failed, and did not complete the task. This was followed by the feminine incarnation of Herzeloyde, the mother of Parzival, an incarnation in which the wealth of knowledge of Julian fell to the background, and other more receptive forces of soul slowly matured. In the next life, that of Tycho de Brahe, the individuality resurrected the earlier faculties of the soul and its deep knowledge in the elaboration of an astronomy that was not only very scientific and precise, but also was truly informed from a spiritual fountainhead.

By speaking of Julian the Apostate, Steiner was subtly introducing a theme that could be overlooked. He was illustrating that initiates experience great difficulties in bringing to life the impulses that well up from their souls in the epoch of the Consciousness Soul (and even earlier, in the case of Julian). In the same lecture, Steiner returned to biographical themes that further evolved the themes of Lecture 1, although the link may be all but apparent. This is where he spoke of the karma that both drew him close to the Cistercians, and at the same time tore him away from them. We will treat this theme separately, since it has many implications.

The main theme of Lecture 5 is the central role of the incarnations of Julian the Apostate/ Herzeloyde/ Tycho Brahe. The lecture leads us to an understanding of how Julian once more recovered the original impetus (of reconciling opposing streams) in the life of Tycho Brahe. This is a theme that continues in the following lectures. Once more Steiner brought a biographical element in presenting the figure of the author Elizabeth Glück (Betty Paoli), whom he considered a friend. This picks up from where he left off in Lecture 4, a theme that is not immediately evident. Describing her lifetime and previous life is what led Steiner to an important conclusion in regard to the Platonists in his time.

In the following lecture, Steiner then proceeded to illustrate how various figures of importance in his own time were inspired from the spiritual world by Julian the Apostate/ Herzeloyde/ Tycho Brahe. Such individuals as Jacob Frohschammer and Friedrich Wilhelm Joseph Schelling received inspirations from that individuality in the spiritual world. Once again Steiner returned to his own biography. He depicted his own complexion of soul, and his difficulty in fully perceiving the reality of the physical world, which accompanied him in his youth and up until his thirties. He also told of his intense moments of loneliness in the Weimar period, before reaching the momentous time of his experience of Christ before the turn of the century.

Lecture 7 introduces a personality who served as the basis for the archetype of Strader in the Mystery Dramas, and who developed his activity in the last third of the nineteenth century. He had been dissatisfied as a Capuchin monk, and later developed a rationalistic Christianity. Steiner inquired back into his previous lives to find why the man could not find his way to a spiritual understanding of Christianity. Strader is a representative of those modern individuals with the intellectual/rational frame of mind, who cannot fully imbue themselves with what comes to them from the planetary spheres when they go through their after-death journey. The reason for that inability lay in a previous lifetime. The Strader prototype is traced back to the Battle of the Minstrels at Wartburg, a contest between the greatest German poets of the times, with the likes of Wolfram von Eschenbach and Walther von der Vogelweide. In that life, the individuality behind Strader was the poet Heinrich von Ofterdingen, who entered the contest against the previously mentioned poets and others. In order to win the contest, which was set at very high stakes, Heinrich had called upon the help of Klingsor, the black magician. In this way, Heinrich had set obstacles to the rightful development of his following life or lives. This tension of soul between what he carried from his past and the new longings that drew him forward was expressed by Steiner thus: "Darkly in the unconscious life of this man, the unchristian cosmology [the one possessed by Klingsor] still showed itself; but in his ordinary consciousness, he evolved a rationalistic Christianity that is not even very interesting." The reason is probably what appears in Steiner's final remarks. "We can study the karma of the cleverest men of the present day (cleverest in the materialistic sense), and we find in general that in former earthly lives, they had something to do with cosmological aberrations into the realms of black magic." This theme forms a continuation (and intensification) of the moral contrast Steiner had introduced in Lecture 2 between the lives of Ludwig Schleich and August Strindberg.

Lecture 8 revolves around the notion of "certain successive earthly lives, such that if we describe them one after another, we are at the same time giving a description of history." Such examples are on the one hand Cardinal Mazarini/ Hertling (German Reich Chancellor); and on the other hand, Soloviev and his previous two incarnations; one at the time of the Council of Nicaea, the later one in the Middle Ages as a woman. In this contrast, Mazarini/ Hertling represents the soul of an individual who cannot find his way anew into incarnation. He seeks to repeat in his later life what he carried of the external circumstances of the previous life. The contrast between the two figures is centered on Mazarini's early stoic, almost cynical, attitude of mind, and Soloviev's earlier incarnation's deep earnestness in the life of thinking, which continued in Soloviev's time.

The whole cycle of *Karmic Relationships*, Volume 4, broadly speaking, treats two very general themes. The first theme is the contrast between those who take an ascending path through their incarnations, and those who take a descending path. The other theme illustrates the difficulties that appear for carrying out our life's intentions at the time of the Consciousness Soul. This is also the central theme of Lecture 9.

Steiner illustrated the above theme with the case of Thomas Campanella in his later incarnation as the Austrian philosopher Otto Weininger. Weininger committed suicide at age twenty-three, because he had arrived at what, in an earlier lifetime, would have been the end of a life-cycle. In the introduction to the lecture Steiner states: "I will now unfold before you a succession of earthly lives of an individuality, which will reveal to you all manner of hindrances that can indeed arise to prevent the carrying of spiritual contents into the present time." In relation to Campanella, Steiner continues: "There rises in the individuality who was Campanella, in his life after death, an extraordinary opposition to what he received in his former lives on earth." Campanella had taken part in conspiracies to free southern Italy from the Spanish, and had been imprisoned for twenty-seven years. Weininger's antipathy for all the spiritual concepts of pre-Christian and Christian times was developed in relation to the soul's bitterness and regret, associated with a difficult time of his previous life. This set of circumstances led to the creation of an undigested etheric-astral island in the soul. It went so far that after death the Campanella soul completely opposed the spirituality he had embraced formerly. The permeation with rationalism and intellectualism happened even in the life between death and rebirth, before the soul reincarnated as Weininger. Steiner concluded, "All this will show you how much spirituality can be latent in a soul; how much can have come together with intellectualism in the supersensible world, toward the age of the Spiritual Soul; and yet it cannot come forth in the present age. Spirituality wants to come forth but cannot, even when the present life is no more than the repetition of a period of life that was lost [the years that Campanella had spent in prison], as it were, in former times." This was the soul's condition that led Weininger to commit suicide just at the time that would have corresponded to the end of his imprisonment, because he felt there was no further possibility for him to live. A new world outlook would have helped the soul enter into a new life—something Weininger did not have the strength to find in the world; hence the despair, which led him to suicide.

Steiner offered the comment that this reaction is in no way unique at the time of the Consciousness Soul. "Now it happened thus with very many souls. Even before their earthly life, while they lived through the age of the Spiritual Soul in supersensible worlds, they became hostile to their former spiritual experience. In effect, it is extremely difficult to carry into a present earthly body what was experienced spiritually in former ages." And Steiner added that this difficulty arises from present-day rationalism and intellectualism.

The carefully built architecture of thought of the lecture cycle culminates in the description of the life and work of Schröer in Lecture 10. Here Steiner alluded to Schröer's task, and how he had been unable to fulfill it. Schröer is the ultimate example of the ideas advanced previously in the cycle. The theme of the unfulfilled tasks of the incarnations of a Julian the Apostate and a Weininger/Campanella reverberated in Steiner's time. Steiner reiterated the difficulties of fulfilling one's task in the epoch of the Consciousness Soul, in an important remark. "We must understand that strength and energy, perseverance, and a holy enthusiasm are necessary to transform into spirituality the intellectualism which, after all, belongs to the present age." Schröer did not find the necessary inner strength for it. Following the example of Weininger, we see that a much more important initiate was also unable to complete his mission.

Considering that Lecture 10 was the next-to-last full lecture Steiner gave, only five days before the famous *Last Address*, we can detect Steiner's sense of urgency in leaving us a spiritual testament. We can apprehend that urgency by what it meant for him to take on Schröer's task, especially if we return to Lecture 1; and if we appreciate Steiner's frustration in being prevented from promoting what was more specifically his task. His intense loneliness in the Weimar period (Lecture 6) may become more fully understandable through this lens. During that period Steiner had devoted most of his resources to furthering the task of anthroposophy at the expense of his own task; he was impelled to it by the weight of world karma that he alone could fully grasp and carry. In the light of all the above, it becomes clearer that Steiner's impulse was delayed not only because of factors internal to the Society, but also because of world karma. In addition, Ita Wegman, who played an important part in all of Steiner's incarnations, entered the fullness of her role only toward the end of Steiner's life. That added delay must have been another formidable burden upon Steiner, even with the devotion and multiplied dedication of Marie Steiner.

In summary, our awe toward Steiner is only increased by this exploration, which leads us to realize that this initiate carried two tasks in parallel for practically his whole life. The first task was the laying out of all the fundamental concepts of anthroposophy, and the articulation of the full impulse of reconnecting modern life to the Mysteries. The second task was a full elaboration of the ideas of karma and reincarnation (a first in modern esoteric teachings) in such a way that they become a perceptible reality in an individual's understanding of life.

We could say (somewhat awkwardly) that anthroposophy on the one hand, and the teaching of karma and reincarnation on the other hand, constitute two separate missions. We are using the word "anthroposophy" here as Steiner meant it when he said that developing it was the task of Schröer. To anthroposophists accustomed to hearing "anthroposophy" as a word that includes everything that Steiner ever offered to humanity, this statement would appear confusing, to say the least. Karma and reincarnation would remain truly incomprehensible without the whole language and thought paradigm developed in anthroposophy. That these are two separate tasks may become apparent from how Steiner spoke about them in various instances. In places,

Steiner spoke of anthroposophy and karma and reincarnation as being at least slightly different concerns.

The above assertion is in keeping with Steiner's assessment that knowledge of the laws of karma and reincarnation is the most singular contribution that anthroposophy has to offer the world. The reformulation of scientific knowledge, the idea of attaining knowledge of the higher worlds, or even Christology (which Steiner developed to unprecedented heights), he adds, are not new developments in the history of human knowledge. Only the esoteric teachings of karma and reincarnation are truly unique.[16]

We will now dwell on another central aspect of Steiner's karma in relation to world karma, which manifested in Steiner's relationship with the Cistercians and some of the order's individual members.

Steiner's Relationship with the Cistercians

Steiner said that among the Cistercians were "the last relics of a striving to awaken Platonism—the Platonic world-concept—in unison with Christianity…."[17] What had lived in the School of Chartres survived, although somehow corrupted, among the Cistercians. Thomas Aquinas had spent the days of his final illness at the Cistercian abbey of Fossanova, and died there. That thread was picked up early in Steiner's life path. Steiner probably had one of his first contacts with the Cistercians through Robert Anderski, a liberal and tolerant priest of the neighboring village of Saint Valentin, who, however, "never spoke of things that usually interest a priest."[18]

While living in Neudörfl, the young Steiner enjoyed going to the monastery of the Most Holy Redeemer, meeting the monks on walks and hoping that they would talk to him, but they never did. "I was in

---

[16] Steiner, *Reincarnation and Karma*, March 5, 1912 lecture. The same is restated in *Karmic Relationships*, Volume 3, July 6, 1924 lecture: "Whatever else we may be studying—be it Nature, or the more natural configuration of human evolution in history or in the life of nations—none of these leads us so high up into the cosmic realms as the study of karma."

[17] Steiner, *Karmic Relationships*, Volume 3, July 13, 1924 lecture.

[18] Steiner, *Autobiography*, note on p. 314.

my ninth year when I became convinced that there were very important matters connected with the tasks of these monks, and that I had to learn what they were. Again, I had innumerable questions, which remained unanswered. Indeed, questions about all kinds of matters made me a very lonely boy."[19] One cannot help but ponder how the life of Aquinas may have been reverberating in the young soul. Thomas was five years old when he had first asked the question about the nature of God to his uncle Sinibald.

During Steiner's schooling in Neudörfl, we know from the *Autobiography*, there was a close connection between the school and the church. The assistant master, Franz Maraz, also played the church organ and took care of the church vestments, ornaments, and sacred objects. Steiner mentioned that "we school boys served at the altar and sang in the choir at masses, requiems, and funerals."[20] This he did until age ten. The ritual and the music left an imprint on his soul; not so the Bible reading and catechism. The service was for him an experience of deep significance. Moreover, he had great reverence for the priest, about whom he said, "The image of this man is deeply engraved in my mind... Of the people I got to know up to my tenth or eleventh year, he was by far the most significant." This is restated a little later in the *Autobiography*: "Until my tenth year I intensively took part in the serving in the church, and this often enabled me to be in company of the priest, whom I revered so deeply."[21]

We may sense the reverberations of the Thomas Aquinas incarnation in all of Steiner's proximity to the order. This thread continued during Steiner's adolescence. We find a last reference to Steiner's preoccupation with what lived on from the Aquinas soul, when, referring to his thinking and [how he was] wanting to develop it, he said,

---

[19] Steiner, *Autobiography*, Chapter 3. Another remnant of the child Steiner/Aquinas's devotional attitude appeared in his statement that he liked to climb a mountain near to home in Neudörfl, to visit a chapel that contained the image of Saint Rosalie. "This chapel was at the end of a walk I often took with my family; later on I loved to go there by myself." (*Autobiography*, Chapter 3)

[20] Ibid, Chapter 5.

[21] Ibid.

I wanted to establish a harmony within myself, between such [unbiased] thinking and religious instruction. This was also vitally important for me at that time. We had excellent textbooks in this particular field. With tremendous devotion, I absorbed from them Dogmatism and Symbolism, the description of the ritual, and church history. I lived in these teachings with great intensity.[22]

Obviously, this phase did not carry further; yet Steiner wanted to draw the reader's attention to it over and over again.

Most of what we will relate now is found in the earlier mentioned Lectures 4 and 5 of *Karmic Relationships*, Volume 4. Where not otherwise noted, I will be referring to those two lectures and highlight in italics relevant sections.

In relation to the Cistercians, Steiner said, "*from my earliest youth, until a certain period of my life*, something of the Cistercian Order *again and again* approached me. Having gone through the elementary school, *I narrowly escaped*—for reasons which I explained in my autobiography, *The Story of my Life*—becoming a pupil in a gymnasium or grammar school conducted by the Cistercian Order. *Everything seemed to be leading in this direction*; but my parents, as I have explained, [in the autobiography] eventually decided to send me to the modern school instead." Here Steiner was obviously stating his own preferences over and against those of his parents. In the autobiography he wrote, "My father intended to prepare me in a suitable way for a position with the railroad. This influenced his decision about whether to send me to the Gymnasium or the Realschule. He finally decided I should be a railroad engineer. Thus he chose the Realschule."[23] Steiner concluded that the choice was not too upsetting to him, as he was still quite young. "At that age, my future position was a matter of indifference to me, as was the matter of whether I should go to the middle school, the Realschule, or the Gymnasium." In Lecture 4 he added a telling remark: "…this [change] was also for very good karmic reasons." But the longing still remained;

---

[22] Steiner, *Autobiography*, Chapter 7.
[23] Ibid, Chapter 6.

in later times Steiner started buying Greek and Latin textbooks and pursued his own classical education, while also tutoring students from the Gymnasium.

There are similar statements in *Karmic Relationships*, Volumes 3 and 6. In Volume 3, Steiner said that "before the Weimar period, I could never escape from the presence, in one way or another, of the Cistercian Order; and yet again I was always somehow kept at a distance from it." And further, "It was a *strange play of forces* that *drew me to them and at the same time held me at a distance*."[24]

The Cistercian influence continued, in spite of Steiner's having gone to modern school. "But the modern school that I attended was only five steps away from the Cistercian grammar school. Thus we made the acquaintance of all those *excellent Cistercian teachers* whose work was indeed of a high quality at the time." Where this relationship went is commented upon later, when Steiner said "*I was deeply attracted to all these priests*, many of whom were extremely learned men. I read a great deal that they wrote and was profoundly stirred by it. *I loved these priests…*"[25] From these premises, he concludes, "*In short, the Cistercian Order was near me. And without a doubt* (though these of course are hypotheses such as one uses only for purposes of illustration), if I had gone to the Cistercian *school I should, as a matter of course, have become a Cistercian*."

That the statement above is not a mere figure of speech is confirmed further by the fact that Steiner wanted to emphasize that the relationship with the Cistercians continued later. After he went to Vienna, he said, "I came into the circle around Maria Eugenia delle Grazie, where many professors of the theological faculty in Vienna used to gather." The circle of delle Grazie met in the home of professor Laurenz Müllner, a liberal-thinking philosopher. The "spiritual center" of the group was formed by the theologian Karl Werner, who had written a famous work on Thomas Aquinas, and whom Steiner never met.[26] Werner also had interest in cosmology; that is, in the relationship between the spheres

---

[24] Steiner, *Karmic Relationships*, Volume 3 July 13, 1924 lecture.

[25] Steiner, *Karmic Relationships*, Volume 6, June 18, 1924 lecture.

[26] Delle Grazie was a key figure of a pessimistic group, formed mainly of Catholic theologians, predominantly Cistercian professors. They met in the home of professor Laurenz Müllner, a liberal-thinking philosopher.

of the planets and the hierarchies. In some way, Werner laid the ground for the recognition of Aquinas's soul in Steiner's life. About this circle of people we hear: "*I learned to know some of them intimately. All those professors were members of the Cistercian Order. Thus once again I came together with the Cistercians,* and *through the currents which flow through the Cistercian Order today,* I have been able to follow many things back into the past." [That is, streams of the Michael School as described in *Karmic Relationships,* Vol. 3.]. Notice that Steiner leads us back to where he started by stressing that his interest lay in *the currents which flow through the order,* not the order itself; in other words, the people whom he met through the order in that time and place in history.

How deep that link was is explained immediately afterward as an example, presumably one of many. Steiner refers to a professor of theology who came to him after he gave a lecture. Steiner commented on what the professor said: "He uttered words in which was contained his memory of *having been together with me in a former life on earth.*" The links that Steiner had with these individuals are deep. This is why the whole of the matter of the Cistercians is closed in this way. "Here you see, I have told you something of *the karmic foundations which have made it possible for me to speak at all in this form about these particular streams.* For one cannot study these things by mere study. One's study of them must consist in life itself." Steiner was referring to the two streams of the Michael School, of which he was speaking in the previous Lecture 3, and in the beginning of Lecture 4; not to mention the whole cycle of *Karmic Relationships,* Volume 3. In that cycle, a clue is offered about the fate of the people of the School of Chartres, which concerns us here. After explaining the autobiographical events of his relationship to the Cistercians, Steiner added: "And to me those things were most important which revealed to me: it is indeed impossible for any of those who were the disciples of Chartres to incarnate at present, and yet it seems as though some of the individualities connected with that School became incorporated, if I may call it so, for brief periods, in some of the human beings who wore the Cistercian garment."[27] Betty

---

[27] Steiner, *Karmic Relationships*, Volume 3, July 13, 1924 lecture.

Glück had been a noticeable exception, but a person who felt out of step with her age. To offer an example of Platonic inspiration, Steiner referred to a conversation he had about the Christ-Being. Here Steiner said, "For the conversation was carried on, not from the present-day dogmatic standpoint of Theology, but from the standpoint of Neo-Scholasticism." Thus, the *currents which flow through the order* are both the Aristotelian and the Platonist. The Aristotelian currents are made clear through the last example, and through the research of Karl Werner into Thomas Aquinas's life. But in the Cistercian stream were also held the last traces of Platonism in the nineteenth century; so much so, that some Platonic souls could occasionally speak through members of the order.

Let us pause to draw attention to the ultimate consequences of what Steiner was calling attention to. He was telling us that here are people with whom he had intimate connections from previous lives; hence, people whose opinions he reads with "keen devotion." From all of this it becomes clear that the statement "I should, as a matter of course, have become a Cistercian," is not a concession to sentimentalism (to which Steiner was not prone). The statement is, in fact, repeated in *Karmic Relationships* Volume 6, "*I should have become a priest in the Cistercian Order.* Of that there is no doubt whatever. ...*I loved these priests* and the only reason why I passed the Cistercian Order by was because I did not attend the Gymnasium."[28] Remember, in passing, that what Steiner said of his later acquaintances and friendships had already been true earlier for the Cistercian Franz Maraz. Steiner was telling us that his inclinations would have drawn him to join with these people, not because they were Cistercians, but because they were "carrying forward old threads of spiritual life which are indeed of the greatest value for Anthroposophy itself." In fact, in regard to the Cistercian Order he said that the "stream of development has become decadent." No, all of this was, or rather would have been, Steiner's karma, had it not been for a larger world karma that was made possible through the intervention of his parents, particularly his father. In the end, "it was all for very good karmic reasons." How important he judged it to be for the members to understand what karma

---

[28] Steiner, *Karmic Relationships*, Volume 6, June 18, 1924 lecture.

was at play, is also restated in *Karmic Relationships*, Volume 6. "In the future, the Anthroposophical Society must learn to understand, with full consciousness, something of its karma."[29]

It was in the circle of the Cistercians that Steiner also learned something important about the fate of the Platonic stream. This transpires most clearly from Steiner's research into the karmic biography of Elizabeth Glück.[30] That leaving this circle of people was a difficult decision is indicated in Steiner's words: "I was now divided between this

---

[29] Ibid.

[30] Most of what we will elucidate here about Elizabeth Glück/ Betty Paoli comes from the lecture of September 14, 1924 in *Karmic Relationships*, Volume 4. In the previous lecture Steiner had just talked about his relationship to members of the Cistercian Order, and that he would have possibly joined the order. In relation to Elizabeth Glück, he prefaces her life by saying that there have been very few incarnations of spirits from the School of Chartres. "I was given one chance of looking back at the School of Chartres through a stimulus in the present," Steiner said in relation to what later was found to be referring to Betty Paoli. He referred to what comes half a page later as "one of those monks, especially devoted to the teachings and works of Chartres, ...after all reincarnated in our time." This was an "authoress who was not only my acquaintance, but my friend." He added that he could speak of her only after the Christmas Conference. From this, we can imagine that he did so because something important lies behind her life story.

The Austrian Elizabeth (Betty) Paoli was born at Vienna in 1814. Her father, a physician, died when she was very young, and the family was left in very poor circumstances. Betty Paoli was compelled to earn her living from early on. For some time she supported herself as a teacher in Russia and Poland. Later, returning to Vienna, she became companion to Princess Marianne Schwarzenberg, a position she held until the death of the Princess in 1848. The following three years Paoli spent traveling, visiting Paris and Berlin, and in 1852 she settled again in Vienna.

Betty Paoli's poems were widely read toward the end of the nineteenth century. Steiner called attention with keen empathy to the fact that the authoress used to repeat that she wanted to die. Steiner adds that this "did not spring from a sentimental or hypochondriac, nay, not even from a melancholic mood of soul." And further, "it was not a question of temperament or melancholy or sentimentality," but that "her whole soul life had ...been dominated by a kind of weariness as the karmic outcome of the mood of soul of yonder monk of Chartres." He connected the depth of the imprint of this previous life to the fact that Betty had maintained a likeness in her facial appearance to her incarnation in the Middle Ages.

house [delle Grazie's], which I so much liked to visit, and my teacher and fatherly friend Karl Julius Schröer, who, after the first visit, never again appeared at delle Grazie's."[31] It is not without interest to note that Steiner devoted all of Chapters 18 and 19 of his autobiography to the circle around delle Grazie, after doing the same for Schröer in all of Chapter 14 and much of 15. In between those, Chapters 15 and 17 speak of Goethe.

Having made these earlier statements about Steiner's originally intended karma, we must repeat that it was with no regret on Steiner's part that his life turned in new directions. On the contrary, Steiner asserts: "I regard it as a very significant and fortunate dispensation of my karma that, while I had been deeply interested in the spiritual world in my early years (in fact, I lived my early life on the spiritual plane), I had not been forced by external circumstances into the classical education of the Gymnasium. All that one acquires through a humanistic education I acquired later on my own initiative...I am glad I was not sent to the Gymnasium in Wiener-Neustadt. I was sent to the Realschule and thus came in touch with teaching that prepared the ground for a modern way of thinking; teaching that enabled me to become closely associated with a scientific outlook."[32]

Steiner went on to tell how the life of Chartres was dominated by a certain twilight mood of the spiritual life. The people of Chartres knew that after their passing, a time would come when ideals would no longer be understood. When she incarnated in modern times, Betty Paoli's soul felt that she had nothing to do with them. Her writings have the same quality; they hardly belong to their time. The mood of the life of Chartres still penetrated in these lines. Steiner concluded: "If her whole life of soul had not been dominated by a kind of weariness as the karmic outcome of the mood of soul of yonder monk of Chartres, I could scarcely imagine a personality more fitted to behold the spiritual life of the present day in connection with the traditional life of the Middle Ages."

Having said all of the above, Steiner pointed once more to the previous picture, in which he had described his experiences with the Cistercian Order, just to stress the link of continuity with what came before in the lecture cycle. This seems to indicate that here was another soul who was part of that circle, maybe through those who moved around the poetess Maria Eugenia delle Grazie. Could it be that here is another soul who would have gravitated around Steiner's circle, had world karma not taken her in another direction?

[31] Steiner, *From Symptom to Reality in Modern History*, November 1, 1918 lecture.
[32] Steiner, *Autobiography*, Chapter 19.

That Steiner went to quite some length to underscore that his inclination and his karmic connections led him one way, but that ultimately, world karma led him another way, must all be for a good reason. And why is this a point of such importance that it was stressed repeatedly? It seems we are here at the intersection of two movements of karma; the first is what Steiner formed of a personal karma, if such it could be called in his case. We may call it, rather, his "normal" karma or the regular karma of evolution. The second, the karma that he accepted wholeheartedly, seems to underscore the necessity of world karma at play. Given that Schröer had given up his world task, it was to be expected that Steiner would "pick it up," for more than one reason. The task of Schröer was far too important for world evolution for an initiate to simply pass it by; moreover, understanding of karma and reincarnation would have been impossible without the foundation of spiritual science.

In the context presented above, a twofold scenario has emerged in Steiner's life. The first, his natural tendency to see his future in Cistercian circles, has the landmark signs of a karma that could have been, but was not to be. World karma required otherwise, and Steiner understood it early on; and he did not oppose it. The second scenario was the karma that unfolded, and is known to history and to all anthroposophists. Within this context, a question has arisen for the author. Steiner indicated, with surprise, that Platonists could not incarnate in his time. Was this also a consequence of world karma?

Coming to the above conclusions allows us to formulate further hypotheses. Given the richness of influences that were somehow preserved in the Cistercian Order, it is a curious fact (to say the least) that, having abandoned his inclinations toward this existing western stream, Steiner later joined the eastern stream of Theosophy. If Steiner's natural inclination and original karmic mission had drawn him in a natural way to circles in which Christianity was taken for granted (the Cistercians), where would Schröer's task have developed? We know that in Plato's soul, the echo of all the pre-Christian Mysteries lived. In Platonic fashion, these survived in the School of Chartres. This complexion of soul would have prepared Schröer to find his way into

Theosophy just as Steiner did, to accomplish what world karma called him to accomplish. The step that appeared as a tremendous sacrifice to Steiner would have been more natural to Schröer.

Very early in life, Steiner had already built up all the soul faculties that equipped him for the fulfillment of his world task. He was able to spiritually research a given individual's previous lives as early as 1888, if not sooner. But signs of destiny had already shown him that something else lay in store for him.

CHAPTER 2

STEINER'S RESEARCH INTO KARMA AND REINCARNATION

We will now attempt to explore what Steiner intended to achieve through the novel introduction of the ideas of karma and reincarnation among his esoteric teachings. To begin, let us retrace Steiner's first steps into karmic spiritual research. We will then draw a timeline of Steiner's efforts in restoring knowledge of karma and reincarnation within the modern Mysteries, and finally, look at the structure of the Mystery Dramas in which the teachings of karma and reincarnation come to life in an artistic manner.

Rudolf Steiner's First Steps into Karmic Spiritual Research

In the time between ages eighteen and twenty-one, Steiner walked the essential steps leading to perception of previous lives, starting with the perception of the eternal "I," so that he was completely equipped for what would have been his life task. By 1888, he was able to find the eternal "I" in its previous embodiments. Let us follow the steps of this inner evolution.

A key event in Steiner's life occurred close to his first Moon Node return. In October 1879, Steiner met with the individual whom he referred to as "the Master," the incarnation of Christian Rosenkreutz.

This occurred at exactly the same time in which the Spirits of Darkness were cast out of the spiritual world into the physical world, and Michael became the time regent. After the meeting with the Master, Steiner did an intensive study of Hegel, and of modern philosophy as it developed in Germany after the 1850s, most particularly what related to the theory of knowledge.[33]

In his *Autobiography*, Steiner mentioned that from early on he was struggling with the concepts of space and time. He had tackled the question of space with his projective geometry studies, through which one can realize that the point of infinity to the right is the same as the one to the left. This relatively easy illustration did not satisfy him; he sought the exact mathematical demonstration of this truth.

Understanding of the reality of time was acquired shortly before the meeting with the Master. "It was at this time—and this belongs already to outward occult influences—that full clarity about the idea of time arose. This insight bore no relation to my studies, and was entirely directed from occult life. It involved the insight that the evolution that advances in a forward direction interacts with a reverse evolution— the occult and astral. This knowledge is the precondition for spiritual vision."[34] In the autobiographical lecture of February 4, 1913, Steiner mentioned that he was introduced by the Master to key ideas about time. The Master used for this purpose a "book that could stimulate one to follow special paths and steps."[35] The book had been frequently censored because of its anticlerical nature.[36]

---

[33] Rudolf Steiner, Notes written for Edouard Schure in Barr, Alsace, September 1907 (also known as "Barr Document") typescript notes.

[34] Steiner, "Barr Document."

[35] Steiner, *Self-Education: Autobiographical Reflections, 1861-1893* February 4, 1913 lecture (Spring Valley, N.Y: Mercury Press).

[36] Hella Wiesberger believes she found this book through the help of Hans Erhard Lauer, with whom Steiner had a conversation about it. Lauer forgot the name of the book and could not find it, but nevertheless remembered something Steiner said about it, which Wiesberger could follow further. She came thus across the work of the Austrian Lazarus B. von Hellenbach, *Die Magie der Zahlen als Grundlage aller Mannigfaltigkeit und das scheinbare Fatum* (*The Magic of Numbers as a Foundation for the Varieties and Probabilities of Destiny*). See Hella Wiesberger: *1879-1882: Années de Genèse de la Science Spirituelle Anthroposophique*, Chapter:

The first direction of time is what we experience in the physical world. The second direction is the stream in which the human being lives after death in the stage of kamaloka: a stream in which time is experienced in reverse. The dual stream of time manifests in the realm of the living in evolution and involution, growth and decay, progression and regression, and in biographical rhythms with expansion and contraction.

In the concept of the threefoldness of the human being—body, soul and spirit—time plays the central part (soul) between the polarities of space (body) and eternity (spirit). Many years later, Steiner connected these concepts with the idea of metamorphosis, independently from Goethe. Thus, this understanding of metamorphosis extends from the realm of nature to the soul and spirit. Hella Wiesberger indicates that the earliest article in which Steiner addressed a scientific explanation of the problem of space and time dates from 1881–82.[37]

At the same time Steiner finished the third chapter of his *Autobiography* (in which he referred to the years mentioned above), he also offered a lecture that inaugurated the cycles of *Karmic Relationships* (lecture of February 16, 1924: "Karma: Esoteric Considerations"). There he referred to that chapter in his *Autobiography*, and recalled his joy in coming across the ideas of projective geometry about the point at infinity. Then he claimed that this idea, when applied to the notion of time and to the human being, leads to knowledge of reincarnation.

The above preliminary steps, already attained by the year 1882, led directly to cognition of that which unites all the aspects of time and space, the true "I." Referring to when he was eighteen, Steiner wrote "My efforts concerning natural scientific concepts had finally brought me to see that the activity of the human 'I' is the only possible starting

"La connaissance du temps, impulsion fondamentale du début de l'investigation anthroposophique" in *Textes Autobiographiques, Rudolf Steiner, suivis d'une étude de Hella Wiesberger*, (Genève, Switzerland: Editions Anthroposophiques Romandes, 1988) 166.

[37] Hella Wiesberger: *1879-1882: Années de Genèse de la Science Spirituelle Anthroposophique*, Chapter: "La connaissance du temps, impulsion fondamentale du début de l'investigation anthroposophique," in *Textes Autobiographiques, Rudolf Steiner, suivis d'une étude de Hella Wiesberger*, 1975, 177.

point for true knowledge..."[38] Thanks to the research of Wiesberger, we can give a very precise date for the self-contemplation of Steiner's eternal being in time and beyond. This is what he described in a letter to a friend, Josef Köck, dated from January 13, 1881, shortly before reaching age twenty:

> Dear and faithful friend, during the night between January 10 and 11, I could not sleep a single instant. Until midnight I had been reflecting on some philosophical matters, and finally I had lain down to rest on my bed. Last year I struggled to verify what Schelling says, 'We all are endowed with the secret and marvelous ability of being able to abstract from the ordeals of our time by withdrawing into the most intimate depth of our being, so that in this immobility, away from all external influences, we can contemplate the eternal in ourselves.' I have always believed, and still believe having clearly discovered in myself this very intimate capacity that I have been sensing for a long time.[39] (translated from the French version by the author).

Perception of the eternal "I" was the precondition for the ability to perceive the reality of reincarnation at work in individual cases. Each incarnation offers only an image in time of the eternal "I." This is why it is important to have an intuition of the eternal "I," in order to research into a person's karma and perceive its constituent expressions. Let us see what this meant practically in the development of the young seer. Initially Steiner could live in intuition in the perception of the eternal individuality; later, through effort, that intuitive cognition could extend to perception of previous lives.

Steiner's social life had a very unusual quality—one he called "leading a double life." Owing to his soul make-up, he found it easy

---

[38] Steiner, *Autobiography: Chapters in the Course of My Life: 1861-1907*, Chapter 13.
[39] Wiesberger, *1879-1882: Annees de Genese de la Science Spirituelle Anthroposophique*, in *Textes Autobiographiques*, 164-165.

to follow all of his friends' interests, but could hardly find anyone who could follow his own, let alone understand them. However, no matter how alone he felt at times, this kind of experience had an important place in his further growth. Steiner's biography is filled with the portraits of friends; many of them had an important, if not exclusive, confidant in him. One is filled with a certain awe at the intimate portraits of the tragic lives of two friends, both of whom the young Steiner followed with keen interest, and assisted as far as he was able. The first is described as "a young man with a wonderful idealism"; the second "in every way the opposite of the fair-haired youth [the first friend]."[40] Steiner was able to enter into another person's soul with the same objectivity with which he pursued Goethean studies. This is how he expressed it later in life: "My powers of observation were directed toward observing, entirely objectively and as an object of contemplation, life as people live it. I scrupulously avoided criticizing what people did, or allowing sympathy or antipathy to influence my relationship with them; my aim was simply to experience the effect on me of a person as he is. I soon discovered that this kind of observation of the world leads us into the realms of the spirit."[41] And, as a consequence, "...I perceived the spiritual world as immediate reality; the spiritual individuality of each person was revealed to me with total clarity.... When people died, I followed them as they journeyed into the spiritual world."[42]

An example will highlight the level at which Steiner's soul communed with other individuals. Steiner had been a friend to a family whose father lived very much as a recluse, so much so that the two had never met. The father was revered and much talked about by those who knew him well. Hearing about him, the young Steiner felt a picture arise in his soul; he was able to say, "Indeed I knew that the man was as close to me in spirit as if I had had extensive contact with him." The sons must have felt Steiner's ability, because they entrusted him with preparing the funeral address and complimented him on his perceptiveness of the departed soul. Thus, without actual physical contact, Steiner had

---

[40] Steiner, *Autobiography*, Chapter 12.
[41] Ibid, Chapter 12.
[42] Ibid, Chapter 51.

communed with the individual's "I."[43] Steiner had reached a very high degree of what we could call today an empathic state.

The young Steiner met a second father in another family that he knew equally well. What this individual had in common with the previous one was his deep immersion in the scientific materialistic worldview of their times. However, the two had not led materialistic lives. Steiner followed them in their journey after death. This is what he said of their souls after death: "The souls of both men (the one I was close to in Vienna and the one I came to know spiritually in Weimar) were magnificently shining spiritual figures after their death; their souls were filled with images of spiritual beings who are connected with the foundation of the world."[44] In the spiritual world they had gained the ability to orient themselves with certainty and discrimination, thanks to their solid scientific thinking. Steiner received from them confirmation of his feelings about scientific thinking and the inner strength to develop his *Philosophy of Freedom*.

About the manner in which his dispassionate observation became an ability to sense and see the reality of previous lives, Steiner further said:

> Such insight [into previous lives] cannot be gained by contemplating a person's immediately obvious expressions, but arises through a study of the traits that seem to accompany such expressions, and in fact, deepen endlessly through intuition. Nor is it useful to try to gain such insight while with the person. Once a strong impression reverberates and becomes like a vivid memory, what is ordinarily considered significant dissolves, and what seems 'insignificant' begins to speak a clear language.[45]

And he stressed the fact that nobody should expect to exert this faculty in an intense personal scrutiny of the individual; this would violate privacy.

---

[43] Steiner, *Autobiography*, Chapter 10.
[44] Ibid, Chapter 47.
[45] Steiner, *Autobiography*, Chapter 20

Let us turn to three key experiences in Steiner's perception of previous lives: two concern other persons, the third concerns Steiner himself. We will first retrace the observations Steiner shared about Franz Brentano— the German philosopher and psychologist—as they came to him in 1879. Steiner had read most of what Brentano wrote. The young Steiner could see a similarity between Brentano's thinking (never breaking through to reality), and his whole bearing. He described Brentano holding a manuscript loosely in his hands as if it might slip from them at any moment. "His expressive 'philosopher's hands' helped me understand his approach to philosophy."[46] These observations are what Steiner described as "points of entry" for deciphering symptoms that point to forces that metamorphose from one life into the next. Whether or not Steiner broke through from the observations noted above, to the perception of Brentano's previous life at that time, is not known. However, Steiner's approach is reminiscent of the method he later adopted, and with which he familiarized his audiences in his *Karmic Relationships* lectures of 1924.

The ability to enter into contact with the individual "I" reaches a step further (at least according to what Steiner reveals in his *Autobiography*) in the figure of Fercher von Steinwand, in the year 1888. The encounter with the poet, who was a bit of a recluse, had occurred upon Steiner's insistence after he had read his poems, which had touched him deeply. Steiner tells us that at this time he had been wrestling further with the idea of repeated earth lives. In the poet he saw clearly someone whose strong individuality could not be explained by his environment. He had been struck by Steinwand's enthusiasm. Steiner felt upon their first encounter, that, although advanced in age, Steinwand really was the youngest of all the people gathered that day. "His facial expression and every gesture revealed to me a soul being who could only have been molded at the time of Greek paganism and its influence on the development of Christianity at the beginning of the Christian era."[47] The

---

[46] Steiner, *Autobiography*, Chapter 10.

[47] Ibid, Chapter 20. Friedrich Zauner has continued the poet's characterization and come to the conclusion, agreed upon by Thomas H. Meyer, that he was the reincarnation of Dionysius the Areopagite. This had played an important part in

meeting with von Steinwand was the prelude to the decisive encounter with Wilhelm Anton Neumann on November 9, 1888, four to five months later.

Neumann was a very learned Cistercian priest, with whom Steiner had many long conversations, including a conversation on reincarnation. Neumann knew quite a bit about the topic but felt uncomfortable discussing it. Steiner related that the personified being of dogmatic Catholicism was present between the two of them; it created an obstacle to a frank conversation, and explained Neumann's reservations. Nevertheless, in the same encounter, Neumann offered Steiner a book about the Druzes in which reincarnation was mentioned.

In 1878, Schröer founded the Vienna Goethe Association, and there, in November of 1888, Steiner gave a lecture on "Goethe as the father of a new aesthetics." After hearing it, Neumann came to Steiner exclaiming, "The seeds of this lecture you gave today are to be found already in Thomas Aquinas!" Steiner referred to this conversation in the lecture on Aquinas of May 24, 1920, where he added, "It was an extraordinarily interesting experience for me to hear from Father Wilhelm Neumann— who naturally was fully conversant with Thomism, since neo-Thomism had already surfaced among the Catholic clergy—that he felt Thomism contained the seed of what I had already put forward as a consequence of Goethe's worldview in relation to aesthetics."[48]

As Thomas Meyer points out, Steiner returned to this connection after the Christmas Foundation Meeting on two occasions. He first mentioned the reference to the experience of his previous earthly life on July 18, 1924. "And then came the remarkable thing that I was giving a lecture on one occasion in Vienna. The same person was present and after the lecture he made a remark that could be understood as the fact that at this moment he had full understanding of a modern human being and his relationship to his former incarnation. And what he said at that moment about the connection between two lives was correct, not wrong.

Aquinas' education. See T. H. Meyer, *Rudolf Steiner's Core Mission: the Birth and Development of Spiritual-Scientific Karma Research*, 44

[48] Rudolf Steiner, *The Redemption of Thinking: A Study in the Philosophy of Thomas Aquinas*, May 24, 1920 lecture.

But he understood nothing at all and was only saying it."[49] Without being fully aware of it, Neumann was the first to offer Steiner a point of departure into knowledge of his last incarnation. Steiner mentioned the fact again in the lecture of September 12, 1924. "...after my lecture ended, he [Neumann] said something very remarkable which I only want to refer to in general: he spoke a phrase which contained a memory of his connection with me in a former incarnation."[50] In a private conversation with Friedrich Rittelmeyer, who wrote it down at the end of the thirties, Steiner commented "...my own former incarnation dawned on me."[51] Clearly, this was not a simple confirmation, but new information. It seems that Steiner had made no attempt to find out about his previous incarnations prior to that time, nor attempted to lay down a theory of karma and reincarnation. Note then how Steiner first perceived other individuals' previous lives, then his own. Furthermore, he was brought to the realization of his own through someone else and not from an egotistic concern. And from the year 1888 onward, Steiner was uniquely equipped to offer humanity a fresh spiritual understanding of the laws of karma and reincarnation.

Due to the events that led to Steiner's having to take up Schröer's task, the introduction of the spiritual-scientific understanding of karma and reincarnation followed an all-but-linear development. In fact, intense phases of elaboration of the theme were followed with periods in which it faded into the background, as we will see next.

Historical Attempts to Introduce the Teachings of Karma and Reincarnation

In *Karmic Relationships* Steiner offered the challenging thought that the Anthroposophical Movement was actually "returning to its own germinal impulse." There he also specified, "Apart from this, I can remind you today of something else. The first few lectures I was to give at that time [1902] to a very small circle were to have the title, 'Practical

---

[49] Rudolf Steiner, *Karmic Relationships*, Volume 8, July 18, 1924 lecture.
[50] Rudolf Steiner, *Karmic Relationships*, Volume 4, September 12, 1924 lecture.
[51] T. H. Meyer, *Rudolf Steiner's Core Mission*, 52.

Exercises for the Understanding of Karma.'"[52] Then Steiner proceeded to confess that he became aware of intense opposition to this proposal and therefore the lectures were not given. He concluded, "Thus we return in a certain sense to the starting point. What must now be a reality was then intention." Let us deepen this exploration further.

The same idea expressed above was brought up throughout the *Karmic Relationships* cycles. In Volume 5 Steiner said, "And now that we have tried through the Christmas Meeting at the Goetheanum to re-organize the Anthroposophical Society, I am able to speak about a certain fact to which probably very little attention has been paid hitherto." And further: "I gave a first lecture which was similar in character to the lectures given later to the groups. This first lecture had an unusual title, one which might at the time have been considered rather daring. The title was 'Studies of the Practical Working of Karma.' My intention was to speak quite openly about the way in which karma works."[53] From the above it appears that at least one lecture was given; none followed.

Much the same is said in *Karmic Relationships*, Volume 6. "At the very first gathering held in Berlin for the purpose of founding the German Section of the Theosophical Society, I chose for a lecture I proposed to give, the title, 'Practical Questions of Karma.' I wanted to introduce then what I intend to achieve now, namely, the serious and earnest study of karma."[54] As to what these lectures and "practical exercises" could be, that is specified in *Karmic Relationships*, Volume 2, Lecture 6. Immediately after introducing what is known as the "Moon/ Sun/ Saturn exercise," Steiner had this to say: "And if one is going to speak of practical karma exercises—I told you already that I wanted to do it at the beginning of the foundation of the Anthroposophical Society, but did not succeed at that time—then one must really begin in this way." This offers us an understanding that Steiner had in mind quite advanced exercises when he initially brought forth his teaching of karma and reincarnation.

Although Steiner conveyed that he did not achieve his goals in the

---

[52] Steiner, *Karmic Relationships*, Vol. 4, September 5, 1924 lecture.
[53] Steiner, *Karmic Relationships*, Vol. 5, March 31, 1924 lecture.
[54] Steiner, *Karmic Relationships*, Vol. 6, April 16, 1924 lecture.

way he had set out to do, he added a telling comment. After saying that his impulse was not taken up, he continued, "It therefore remained a task which had to be pursued under the surface, as it were, of the anthroposophic stream, performed as an obligation to the spiritual world."[55] Even after the false start of 1902, Steiner had brought up his karmic research here and there. Already in the lecture of October 18, 1903, he mentioned that Copernicus was the reincarnated Cardinal Cusa.[56]

We can distinguish three phases, or waves, in Steiner's attempts to bring out the teachings about karma and reincarnation together with the practical exercises—although traces exist also in between these phases. The first was the above-mentioned isolated attempt as early as 1902, from which Steiner soon desisted.

The second wave occurred in conjunction with the performing of the Mystery Dramas. Lectures about karma and reincarnation followed in their wake, most intensely from 1910 to 1913, then later with isolated lectures. These include the cycles *Manifestations of Karma* (1910) and *Reincarnation and Karma* (1912); the comments on the Mystery Dramas present in *Secrets of the Threshold*; and those gathered in *Three Lectures on the Mystery Dramas*. In 1910 Steiner also gave the cycle of lectures on *Occult History*, in which he followed individuals from one incarnation to the next. In the backdrop of the whole cycle lie the figures of Eabani and Gilgamesh, Aristotle and Alexander the Great, through which he was pointing back to his own incarnations and those of Ita Wegman. These lectures could be called the first karma cycle, although they were given in a veiled fashion; Steiner did not explicitly point to the individualities of the present. Steiner's second effort came to an end with the onset of World War I.

The years 1909–1910 were pivotal years for the revelations streaming from the spiritual world through Steiner. In addition to giving us the first Mystery Drama, these years are marked by the first lectures mentioning the reappearance of Christ in the etheric, and the first revelations about the Fifth Gospel (starting from the *Gospel of Saint*

---

[55] Steiner, *Karmic Relationships*, Vol. 5, March 31, 1924 lecture.
[56] Steiner, lecture of October 18, 1903, not translated.

Luke with the revelations about the two Jesus children). And the drama, *The Portal of Initiation,* was inaugurated, with the vision by the seeress Theodora of the coming of Christ in a new form.

The fact that Steiner gave the first karma exercises in lectures given in the years 1911-12 is of great importance for our study.[57] It seems that initially Steiner was still tentative, maybe knowing how much the ground needed to be prepared to overcome the resistances he had met in 1902 with the first attempt. In one of the lectures he spoke about how to work on the soul life in the realm of concepts and thinking, emotions and will. Regarding the latter he says the insight that "The most beneficial influence on our will is exerted by a life wholly directed towards comprehending human karma. We might also say a soul life which strives to develop, as its primary characteristics, serenity and acceptance of our destiny. And what better way can one find of developing this acceptance, this calmness of soul in the presence of one's destiny, than by making karma an actual content in one's life."[58] Within the lecture he illustrates how to face one's sorrow and one's joys. Pain and sorrow are usually deserved, and the cause is either in this life or in the previous. And to this we need to respond by inwardly conducting ourselves with this specific understanding, and by promoting acceptance of destiny. Meanwhile, joy most often points to the future, not to the past. "When we investigate karma by occult means, we always discover that in most cases joy has not been earned, and we should accept it gratefully as sent to us by the gods, as a gift of the gods." This should motivate us to apply what comes to us as joy usefully for the good of our fellow human being. Acceptance of our karma, made a reality as in the two instances above, strengthens our will. Reactions of anger or depression rob us of vitality. What was still a general injunction or a desired attitude in 1911 evolved into more specific exercises in 1912. We will return to these later in the chapter.

---

[57] Steiner, *Esoteric Christianity and the Mission of Christian Rosenkreutz,* "Jeshu ben Pandira and the Christ Impulse," November 5, 1911 lecture; "The Dawn of Occultism in the Modern Age," January 29, 1912 lecture; and "The True Attitude to Karma," February 8, 1912 lecture.

[58] Steiner, *Esoteric Christianity,* November 5, 1911 lecture.

Steiner's continued effort on the Mystery Dramas was prevented by the outbreak of World War I. About this he said,

> I will try to give a brief outline of what was to have been the content of the Munich lectures; but the most important and essential information that was to have been given there must be reserved for less turbulent times. I am astonished to find certain people thinking that the strenuous efforts required for giving very important teachings of Spiritual Science (as was intended in Munich), can be applied in times such as those in which we are now living. But it will be realized one day that this simply is not possible; that the highest truths cannot be communicated when storms are raging. As far as my theme is concerned, I will give a course of lectures on it later on, when karma permits, in substitution for what was to have been given in Munich.[59]

The stream of karma revelations decreased considerably, and fully resumed only after the Christmas Conference. The final attempt, which was only partial because of Steiner's premature death, took place after World War I, and most strongly after the Christmas Conference. And the reason for this is the following, according to Steiner:

> There were mighty followers of Michael...but also mighty demonic powers, which, under the influence of Ahriman, opposed what was meant to come into the world through Michael. ...And each time, even after having experienced and lived with these questions for decades, it was nevertheless as though, if you tried to express these things, then the enemies of Michael always came and stopped you from speaking. [But] recently it has become possible to speak about these things...Now the connections between earth lives can be discussed

---

[59] Steiner, *Occult Reading, Occult Hearing*, Oct. 3, 1914 lecture.

openly. This is linked to the revelation of the Michael
Mysteries...What has happened is that the demons
which previously prevented things from being voiced
have been forced into silence.[60]

The lectures on karma and reincarnation form Steiner's single most
important contribution after the Christmas Conference—seventy-five of
them in *Karmic Relationships* alone. There, specific karma exercises were
proposed once again, and this time more fully. In addition, the ideas of
karma and reincarnation acquired a sense of concreteness with specific
references to historical figures, whom Steiner followed throughout their
incarnations. The Christmas Conference itself was framed around the
revelations of the spiritual genesis of the Michael stream, within which
the souls of Aristotle/ Steiner and Alexander the Great/ Wegman played
a central role. Added to this was the repeated injunction to take pains
to figure out which of the Michaelic streams each one of us belongs
to, particularly the polarities of Platonic/ Aristotelian and Old/ Young
Souls.

Notwithstanding the fact that there was a major new development
in 1924, as we will see later, Steiner had already laid the foundations for
what might be called "practical karma work" in the years 1911-12.

Why was Steiner putting such an effort into placing the teachings of
karma and reincarnation prominently within the body of esoteric
revelations? The reasons are clearly stated here and there throughout
his work.

The first reason can be sought in the historical hiatus during which
knowledge of karma and reincarnation had fallen into oblivion, even
within the esoteric schools, although exceptions had been made for
the highest levels of initiation. Aristotle had taken pains to confine
the human being's gaze to this life and this life only. The present times
call for a reversal of this stance. "Now, however, we face a reversal of
the situation [referring to the times in which we could not know about
karma and reincarnation]: we have reached the point where we can make

---

[60] Steiner, *Karmic Relationships*, Volume 8, August 12, 1924 lecture.

no advance unless we turn our gaze to reincarnation. Now is the time when spiritual beings wishing to bring humanity the consciousness of repeated earthly lives have to wage a hard fight against those who would allow only old elements and impulses to enter human consciousness."[61]

And research into karma is of great importance for understanding the way in which all aspects of spiritual reality are encompassed in human biography. "Whatever else we may be studying—be it nature, or the more natural configuration of human evolution in history or in the life of nations—none of these leads up as high into cosmic realms as the study of karma. The study of karma makes us altogether aware of the connections between human life here upon earth and that which goes on in the wide universe."[62] And the importance of the teachings of karma and reincarnation is such that they acquire tremendous practical relevance. This is why Steiner enjoins us to consider with great seriousness his exercises in relation to questions that grow out of our own biographies. "I have often said that the more intensely we penetrate the karmic connections, the more do we see the true essence of freedom. We need not, therefore, fear that by entering into the karmic relationships more accurately we shall lose our open and unimpaired vision of the essence of human freedom."[63]

Knowledge of Higher Worlds and Mystery Dramas

Steiner's Mystery Dramas portray how individuals affect the destinies of one another across various incarnations. Steiner attributed great importance to these plays, so much so that he repeatedly stated that if those plays had been taken more seriously, he would not have had to give as many lectures.[64]

The Portal of Initiation was written in 1910. In this first Mystery Drama, which he calls a Rosicrucian drama, Steiner acknowledged a debt to Goethe's *Fairy Tale of the Green Snake and the Beautiful Lily*. The

---

[61] Steiner, *How Can Mankind Find the Christ*, January 1, 1919 lecture.

[62] Steiner, *Karmic Relationships*, Volume 3, July 6, 1924 lecture.

[63] Ibid, August 4, 1924 lecture.

[64] Steiner, *Three Lectures on the Mystery Dramas*, September 17, 1910, and October 31, 1910 lectures.

second, *The Soul's Probation*, was inspired by the traditions, legends, and underlying historical connections to the Knights Templar. In both plays, Steiner also carried further the inspiration of a pupil who had intended to write the plays. She had died and continued to inspire Steiner from the spiritual world. This is why the first two plays carry the phrase "through Rudolf Steiner." The last two, *The Guardian of the Threshold* and *The Souls' Awakening*, were the fruit of Steiner's inspiration alone.

All through the Mystery Dramas, we see how individuals help each other in the steps of spiritual development. For the first time on stage, a drama offered understanding of human development from a spiritual perspective moving beyond life on earth alone. The characters portray the struggle to follow a spiritual path and apprehend the reality of the spiritual world. This leads them, in turn, to experiences in the soul world; the encounter with the Guardian of the Threshold; the reawakening of memories from the sphere of the Sun and from the Cosmic Midnight; and finally, the reawakening of memories of previous lives. Throughout the play, individuals tied by strong links of destiny play a role in each other's development. Love and willingness for self-sacrifice play a central part in each play.

Many situations of conflict arise throughout the plays and the plot reveals the deeper roots of the conflicts in previous lives. Some conflicts are thus brought to a denouement while others arise and are left open to future resolution. The fourth play ends without a final resolution. Steiner planned further plays, but the tragic circumstances of World War I and the illness leading to his death prevented the continuation of this artistic pursuit.

In the first play we witness the spiritual awakening of the individual Thomasius (also called Johannes). The second drama focuses primarily on the trials undergone by Capesius's soul; the third and fourth follow most closely the fate of Strader. Throughout all the plays, each character continues his own soul development in such a way that a collective maturation culminates in the fourth play, where an attempt is made to bring spiritual knowledge into the world as a renewing impulse, through a project in the economic realm that the group attempts to carry out. The three individuals mentioned, plus Maria, form the nucleus of this endeavor. They can attempt such a step by virtue of the fact that they have harmonized their karma to quite an extent. Offering spiritual guidance to all of them is the figure of the initiate Benedictus. In Scene 9 of *The Guardian of the Threshold*, Benedictus expresses the extent to which these souls have united: "United with you [Capesius], Strader and Thomasius in future will be able to accomplish much for the right progress of men. The forces of soul which they possess have been prepared since earth's beginning in such a way that in the cosmic course, they can unite now with your spirit to form a triad filled with strength."

The four plays constituted something quite novel and unique in the development of anthroposophy; that has been intuited by more than one of Steiner's followers. Interestingly, Ehrenfried Pfeiffer and Valentin Tomberg similarly placed the plays on the same level with Steiner's main books—*The Philosophy of Spiritual Activity: A Philosophy of Freedom; Knowledge of Higher Worlds;* and *Occult Science.*[65] The Mystery Dramas form a contrast and a complementary step to the basic books. *The Philosophy of Freedom* addresses primarily the matter of individual knowledge and moral imagination. The other two basic books (and especially *Knowledge of Higher Worlds*) characterize the archetypal path of development that an individual follows in reaching for spiritual knowledge. Steiner later revealed that what is said in that book in relation to individual development is a valid generalization. However, no individual development follows such an exact blueprint, and there can be great departures from the ideal.

The Mystery Dramas give us an indication of how an individual's development deviates from the idealized and general path given in the basic books. This is supported by what Steiner said: "Everything you find in my book, *Knowledge of the Higher Worlds and Its Attainment,* . . . combined with what was said in *Occult Science,* can be found, after all, in a much more forceful, true-to-life, and substantial form in the Rosicrucian Mystery [*The Portal of Initiation*]. The reason is that it is more highly individualized. In the last analysis, there is no

---

[65] Valentin Tomberg, *Group Work Articles,* and Ehrenfried Pfeiffer, *On Rudolf Steiner's Mystery Dramas,* November 14, 1948 lecture.

such a thing as a 'universal' path of development. There are only the individual forms that this takes."[66]

There is a further difference between the two sets of books. The Mystery Dramas offer us indications of what is needed in order to reach deeper understanding and action in community matters. Through the Mystery Dramas we are given concrete examples of what can be achieved through the concerted action of individuals for the good of the community. This polarity of individual/community is made manifest in how one and the other sets of books are used. *Philosophy of Freedom* and *Knowledge of Higher Worlds* are to be read and studied by the individual, even if supported by a study group. The Mystery Dramas are meant to be performed before an audience, mirroring their intended use in community-building of a new kind. We can experience the plays at progressive depths by reading, seeing, performing, or directing them. And in the performance of the dramas, people come together in ways that stimulate their further development.

Through the Mystery Dramas, especially when performed, we gain insights into the soul life of very diverse individuals. In this way the plays educate our empathy and capacity to gain insight into the reality of other souls. They give another value to knowledge that is gained not only through personal effort, but also through the effects of personal relationships. The characters of the Mystery Dramas gain new insights through the lively interplay, dialogue, and debate with others. They learn to explore the one-sided opinions of others in order to enrich their own one-sided perspectives. This is because these new perspectives can only emerge and be reflected by other people, not abstractly.

Two examples will suffice here. At the beginning of the first play, we see Theodora entering a trance-like state and revealing the new experience of the Christ in the etheric. This is a phenomenon that Strader cannot deny, and it shakes loose the materialistic scientific outlook that has supported him in his vocation. Theodora plays a growing part in his life, first as a friend, then as his wife, leading him to renew his scientific

---

[66] Steiner, *Secrets of the Threshold*, August 29, 1913 lecture.

efforts toward the integration of what spiritual science reveals to be possible.

Capesius is the historian trained in the prevailing materialistic predicament, trying to come to terms with the views professed by the initiate Benedictus. He has difficulty entering the kind of language and ideas that he finds through Benedictus. An awakening occurs to Capesius when the artist Thomasius, with whom he is closely associated, completes his portrait. Capesius is struck by the painting because it seems to bring to life a spiritual perception of his individuality. Thomasius has indeed understood the powers that Capesius had in a previous incarnation, even though they cannot manifest in the present.

Characters in the Mystery Dramas strive to reach to the conscious awakening of the Spirit Self through which we can start to master the impulses of our lower nature. This awakening is an attempt that often takes longer than a lifetime. Among the characters in the play, only Benedictus and Maria have fully attained this level. However, an intermediate stage can be achieved, through which we can assume tasks of a spiritual and social nature while exerting mastery over our lower nature, as is the case for Thomasius toward the end of the dramas.

We will now turn to modern approaches to the question of karma and reincarnation from an anthroposophical perspective before returning to Steiner and reframing the question from a larger perspective.

CHAPTER 3

MODERN ANTHROPOSOPHICAL APPROACHES TO KARMA AND REINCARNATION

The path of the Mystery Dramas can be characterized as a "social path," in contrast to the more individual path outlined by Steiner in *Knowledge of the Higher Worlds*. In the last decades within anthroposophic circles, a longing for a deeper understanding of what we could call a social path has come to the surface of consciousness, and found expression in the work of a number of researchers and authors. Bernard Lievegoed was long a pioneer in this field, offering many practical applications throughout his life. The expression of the uniqueness of this path is clearly articulated in his books *Towards the 21ˢᵗ Century: Doing the Good* (1972), and *The Battle for the Soul* (1993), among others. Other contributions to the matter have been those of Sergei Prokofieff (*The Occult Significance of Forgiveness*, 1991); Margreet van den Brink (*More Precious Than Light: How Dialogue Can Transform Relationships and Build Community*, 1994); Harry Salman (*The Social World as Mystery Center*, 1998); Baruch Luke Urieli and Hans Müller-Wiedemann (*Learning to Experience the Etheric World: Empathy, the After-Image and a New Social Ethic*, 1998); Dieter Brüll (*The Mysteries of Social Encounters*, 2002); and Coenraad van Houten, (*Practising Destiny*, 2000, and *The Threefold Nature of Destiny Learning*, 2004). Apart from Lievegoed's first book, all of these contributions appeared within thirteen years of each other! A real yearning began manifesting at the turn of the century for a deeper understanding of what it is to be social from an anthroposophical perspective.

We will proceed by referring to what various authors have to offer in this field. Progressively, we will move from the sum of the partial vistas opened by these approaches, back to what unites them all in Steiner's legacy. Although we will refer primarily to the social path, on occasion we will bring forward particular "applications" or tools of social development, particularly those contributed by van Houten and van den Brink.

The Path of Forgiveness

Prokofieff takes his start from an understanding of the act of forgiveness.[67] He characterizes the four initial stages of the path of forgiveness as a progressive permeation of the human sheaths by the ego. In the first stage the ego acts upon the physical body; in the second upon the etheric body, in the third upon the astral, and finally the ego acts upon itself. The further stages on the path of forgiveness lie in the distant future, and will not interest us at present. Each of the four steps corresponds in its way to an equivalent step along the Rosicrucian path, the "path of knowledge through the will."

The first stage is achieved through an education of the senses toward tolerance, through the ego's working on the physical body. Through the impressions of the senses, the ego comes to awareness. Consider the case of someone for whom we have only instinctual antipathy. As soon as our senses perceive this person, an immediate, automatic reaction colors our perception. In *Knowledge of Higher Worlds* we encounter the following injunction: "If I encounter a human being and blame him for his weaknesses, I rob myself of the power of higher knowledge; but if I try to enter lovingly into his qualities, I master this power." In the first instance (pure antipathy), we receive the impressions of the sense world through our double. In the second instance, we develop interest

---

[67] Sergei O. Prokofieff, *The Occult Significance of Forgiveness.*

in the other person through a power that transcends sympathy and antipathy. This is tolerance, or what corresponds to the relatively recent term, *empathy*. To achieve this goal, we need to educate the senses from the ego, rather than receiving sense impressions through our double.

Developing the power of empathy through an exertion of the will demands that we see in the other person precisely what is common with ourselves and with the universally human, even before we recognize what makes the other person unique. Tolerance for the other person comes in great part from tolerance toward ourselves; and this is a first step in the recognition of the forces of evil expressed in our soul through our double. This first stage corresponds in the Christian Rosicrucian path to the study of spiritual science, leading to the education of the senses and the transformation of thinking.

The second stage is that of forgiveness proper, to which tolerance/ empathy forms the prelude. In this stage, we work from our ego into the ether body. The stage of forgiveness is rendered possible through the active permeation of our ego by the Spirit Self. Through forgiveness, Christ himself as the Lord of Karma can work in the etheric form.

True forgiveness is a potentized act of tolerance—tolerance that penetrates deeper into the will. Forgiveness obliges us to pass through an experience of inner and outer powerlessness. This is what allows the forces of the lower ego to withdraw. Through repeated effort, the higher ego can assert itself over the lower ego. Since it is possible to forgive only by connecting to our Spirit Self, we need to resort to a discipline that connects us to it, hence to repeated exertions of the will. That some people may be able to do that without a particular discipline simply means that they are already sufficiently imbued and inspired by the Spirit Self in their ego, through grace resulting from previous incarnations.

As the ego needs the sense organs of the physical body, so does the Spirit Self need the organs of perception of the etheric body. There, the Spirit Self can help dissolve the structures of the doubles (partly etheric and astral). In forgiving, we liberate the destructive and darkening elements in our etheric body, initiating a conscious work upon our double. Outwardly, through forgiveness, we act one step more deeply into the Mysteries of evil in our time. We send back into the world as much goodness as it was robbed of by the evil act. This work upon the etheric body may not at first form the suprasensory organs of perception, but it can make us receptive to the macrocosmic forces that emanate from the Christ. On the basis of the examples he studied, Prokofieff concludes, "The path of forgiveness is the most direct and surest path whereby the spiritual forces of the etheric Christ may flow into modern earthly civilization, while the person himself is sooner or later enabled to gain a clairvoyant experience of Him."[68]

Forgiveness is prepared with self-forgiveness that can take various forms. Forgiveness toward self or "toward the spiritual world" comes in one way through the acceptance of blows of destiny. These most often call us to acceptance of a choice we made in the spiritual world (at the Cosmic Midnight) before descending into incarnation. But self-forgiveness extends to all acts, small or large, that we have generated in this life, and that we regret. Through the Mystery Dramas and elsewhere, Steiner calls attention to the essential and productive attitude of *remorse*. Remorse that mourns our shortcomings sets us on the path to self-improvement. By contrast, remorse tied to the idea of our lost perfection is egotistic, and will only generate guilt and hinder our further development. With remorse we balance the past; with forgiveness we prepare the future. The second stage of forgiveness corresponds to the attainment of imaginative knowledge in the Christian Rosicrucian path.

In the third stage of the path of forgiveness, we endeavor to take the karma of another individual or group upon ourselves, allowing the ego to act upon our astral body. A step on the way to this goal lies in developing a sense of responsibility for the actions of fellow human beings or groups/institutions. In moving from forgiveness to taking on the karma of other people or a group, we rely on the help of the Life Spirit. This third stage corresponds to inspiration knowledge in the Christian Rosicrucian path.

In the fourth stage of the path of forgiveness, we participate in bearing the karma of the whole of humanity. It is the stage in which the ego can act consciously upon itself. Steiner's life illustrates this stage along the path. What Steiner as initiate tried to offer through his

---

[68] Prokofieff, *The Occult Significance of Forgiveness*, 55.

life was a true regeneration of the cultural sphere, a regeneration of the power of thinking, offered to the whole of humanity. In order to achieve this task he had to endure opposition from all directions, and develop enormous capacity for forgiveness and sacrifice. At this stage of the path we reach the revelation of Christ in the higher spiritual world. The initiate thus perceives Christ out of his own ego, as the archetype of his ego. This corresponds to the stage of intuitive knowledge in the Christian Rosicrucian path.

The way in which Prokofieff outlines the four stages is illustrated in the Mystery Plays. Let us find a few pointers to this correspondence. In the Mystery Plays, tolerance appears in the initial stages of development through the acceptance of other viewpoints in life. It comes more naturally in Thomasius's ability to experience in his soul the different viewpoints of the individuals that surround him. It forms the center of an intense inner struggle in Capesius and Strader, who were profoundly influenced by the materialism reigning in modern institutions of learning. Among all the characters they were those who most needed to educate their senses.

Forgiveness is rarely mentioned in the plays, or not at all. In its place two other ideas are highlighted. Much of what we call forgiveness is shown as the need to embrace our karmic obligations. Seeing from the perspective of karma and reincarnation, we could talk of *atonement*. Maria and Thomasius are atoning in the present life for the results of decisions they made in their two previous incarnations—the Templar and the Egyptian. Maria, in particular, shows a complete readiness to amend the consequence of decisions in earlier lives. Thus, for example, she realizes the need to support Capesius, whom she had worked to estrange from Thomasius' soul in the Middle Ages.

Where true forgiveness is called upon, the Mystery Dramas speak of *soul sacrifice*. This attitude is present in Theodora, both in her Templar life and in the present. Not surprisingly, she is the one who can announce the coming of the etheric Christ—albeit in a trance-like state of consciousness. Maria takes on soul sacrifice for the sake of those she has joined in previous lives. The higher ego in the act of forgiveness moves toward an active remembrance of the pre-birth resolves taken at the Cosmic Midnight, which come in as flashes, and are soon forgotten, in that sphere and in this life. Maria also takes soul sacrifice a step further in the last play. When Capesius and Thomasius fall short of their commitment, she knows that she has to take all the more responsibility, and step in for both of them.

At a still higher level lies the cooperation between the Brothers in the Council. Here are individuals who have taken tasks and responsibilities for larger groups of human beings or for the whole of humanity. The decisions that are made in the Temple are reached in a completely dispassionate mode. They do not derive from personal preference, but are offered in response to a call from the spiritual world, out of an inescapable inner necessity.

What the Mystery Dramas add to Prokofieff's analysis of the path of forgiveness is the weight that knowledge of previous lives plays in this process. Of course forgiveness can be offered without that knowledge, either through the presence of a strong Spirit Self, or through the education of the will that supports it. However, the central message of the Mystery Dramas is that a karmic lesson is truly learned when the soul can reach objective knowledge about what seems to be a purely subjective matter, one's biography. The example of Maria and Johannes is quite enlightening from this perspective. Through the four plays, we are offered the picture of their previous Templar incarnation, and inklings of their connection through the Mysteries of Hibernia. However, the root causes for their conflicts and shortcomings lie farther back, in the Egyptian incarnation, of which we learn only in the last play. The first revelations are rungs of a ladder, in that they help the two to move further in their spiritual development. The denouement cannot occur through the previous revelations alone; the last tableau of the Egyptian initiation is necessary for a permanent result and change.

Whether we approach reconciliation from the act of forgiveness, or from the perspective of atonement generated by the understanding of our deeper essence in our previous lives, we find many commonalities in the common goals attained. The path of forgiveness and the path indicated in the Mystery Dramas ultimately call us to reorder and harmonize our karma by affecting our perception of the world, and through the contributions that originate in our deeds. In this, they correspond to what Prokofieff characterizes as the "path of the will through thinking," the education of the will that acts in the fulfillment of our karma through the ordering effect of thinking.

We can say that on the Rosicrucian Path we educate our thinking through the will, whereas we strengthen our will through thinking in the path of forgiveness. In the first, we aim at rendering our thinking truly free. In the second, we aim at liberating our will from the constraints to which the double binds it. In concluding, Prokofieff compares the two paths to the two serpents around the caduceus of Mercury. He points out that the Rosicrucian path helps us cultivate the inner life. The path of forgiveness is directed primarily to a cultivation of the outer forms of life. This is precisely what was cultivated in the communities that absorbed the teachings of Manichaeism, the Cathars and Albigenses; and in great measure it was cultivated by the Templars. All these communities created shining examples of what it means to forgive on the Christian path.

Other authors have given weight to the idea of a social path. We will refer here to two of them, Harry Salman and Margreet van den Brink, in order to bring out new elements that characterize this path, which is the same that Prokofieff explores.[69] In addition we will look at a practical tool on this path, which can be characterized as a "counseling conversation" (author's terms).

The Path of Social Development

Ever since the end of the nineteenth century, because of humanity's collective crossing of the threshold, the world-stage is taking the place of the precinct of the Mysteries. Modern life can be understood as a collective Mystery Drama.

The individual path (of cognition) leads us first to the Lower Guardian, who shows us our true nature. It is the path that Steiner outlined in *Knowledge of Higher Worlds*. The path of social development leads us first

---

[69] Harry Salman, *The Social World as Mystery Center: The Social Vision of Anthroposophy*, and Margreet van den Brink, *More Precious Than Light: How Dialogue Can Transform Relationships and Build Community*.

to the Higher Guardian, through whom we can have inklings of the true being of the other and the nature of our collaboration. Consequently, we are thrown back to the Lower Guardian, in the awareness of the distance between the goal to achieve and the obstacles presented by our lower nature.

The social path awakens through the perception of the suffering of others. Here we cross the threshold when we "fall asleep to the other" in an archetypal social phenomenon, of which we will say more later. It is the other human being who leads us into the spiritual world. We can thus learn to perceive our own double when we reach for the place in which the Christ unites us with the other.

Van den Brink also calls the path of social development the "path of the crisis." She sees that the path of social development is the stage in which the individual path to the Christ, first in thinking then in feeling, finally enters into the will. The social path gives "form and content" to the personal path and manifests in our actions. It is a path in the realm of morality.

Van den Brink's analysis allows us to move further into the social path through her practical application of it in the realm of dialogue. Nowadays the need for this path through dialogue is recognized in the fact that we are all longing to be seen, heard, and understood by others; we want to awake to our higher self in the way that often happens when another person hears us fully. However, we are aware both of our inability to hear other people fully, and of our fear, because the first experience is that of an encounter with our double leading us to the Lesser Guardian of the Threshold. On the other hand (and almost by definition), we do not possess innate social skills. We can only cultivate them with patience. Therefore, we can offer support, whether professionally or personally, only once we have both mastered the art of dialogue, and experienced a measure of personal encounters with the Guardian.

Essentially, the dialogue that anyone with communication skills can offer is a path through the layers of the soul from matter (the experiential level) to spirit awareness. In order for this path to reach completion, we must reclaim awareness of our experiences—raise them from the forgetfulness that comes from not having fully digested them, and ultimately let them sink into our unconscious. The listener will help us free these memories, and will allow us to reconnect with our pre-birth intentions as well. For this path to be true and fruitful, it is important to let the experiences speak for themselves, rather than to impose an intellectual layer of interpretation. Going from bodily experience to spirit awareness means moving through the layers of the soul, from the oldest layer (sentient soul) to the youngest (consciousness soul).

In the sentient soul (the soul of experience), we first live through our sense perceptions, our subjective needs, emotions, impulses of the will—in short, the subjective stratum for our perception of the world. We become aware of ourselves inwardly. The second layer of the soul is the heart/mind soul. Through it we can reflect on our experiences, and discriminate between the essential and the nonessential. We become intellectually and emotionally aware. In the consciousness soul, we acquire a deeper perspective on the importance of our experiences, of their truth and inner essence, and place these experiences in relationship to each other.

The above processes are amplified in deep and empathic conversation. To do this, we have to go through the various layers of the soul without skipping stages. Let us deepen what we have briefly outlined. We start from the sentient soul by retrieving the experience as clearly as possible. Through this we relive our fears, sorrow, pain or pleasure, and enthusiasm. This is the first level of connection of the "I" with the Spirit Self. This essential connection is bypassed if we try to move on to intellectualizing before re-experiencing. We will not be able to move further if we do not reach the sentient soul first. We can then look back upon the experiences, discriminating between the essential and the non-essential; forming tentative hypotheses and conclusions. In this way, we dwell in our intellectual soul. At this stage another difficulty arises: that of being able to let go of the fruits of our intellect. We need to sacrifice our earthly thinking. In effect, the next step is better taken after we let the whole content thus elaborated sink down and ripen within our soul. We then connect with the consciousness soul and we receive the previously elaborated content in the form of insights, answers, and a feeling for the deeper truth at a spiritual level. These are more than intellectual or speculative results. In the consciousness soul, we distill an extract of the particular experience.

Having moved from ideas about the path to a specific approach, we will now move into another of these techniques, developed by Coenraad van Houten. The Dutch author and researcher has been looking at the complementarity of his two approaches of "Adult Learning" ("the learning to learn process")[70] and "Destiny Learning"[71] in order to add further aspects of the path of the will through thinking. There is a third path present in van Houten's work—that of "spiritual research"—which is the culmination of adult education and destiny learning, which should not cloud the issue here.[72] Spiritual research itself is attained only through the integration of the first two paths.

Destiny Learning as a Moral Technique[73]

Both Adult Learning and Destiny Learning are based on the exploration of the seven life processes. Steiner has offered us the image of our twelve senses, five known outer senses and another seven more refined senses, as windows through which our soul looks out at the world. Through all the senses pulse the life processes. What the senses let through is further elaborated, turned into a living experience through the life processes.

The seven life processes are breathing, warming, nourishing, secreting, maintaining, growing, and reproducing. There is a process of breathing, of warming, of nourishing, and so forth, for the sense of sight, for hearing, for balance, and so forth. Likewise, every life process affects each of the twelve senses. The first three processes, breathing, warming, nourishing, reach us from the external world. The process of secreting concerns assimilation, absorption, and excretion; it is the turning point of individualizing what is received from the external environment. What is taken from the world by the organism is then transformed in the last three, more inner processes, which sustain first maintenance, then growth, and finally reproduction.

In a human being the life processes are at work in the first three cycles

---

[70] Coenraad van Houten, *Awakening the Will: Principles and Processes in Adult Learning.*

[71] van Houten, *Practising Destiny, and The Threefold Nature of Destiny Learning.*

[72] van Houten, *Creative Spiritual Research: Awakening the Individual Human Spirit.*

[73] van Houten, *Practising Destiny,* and *The Threefold Nature of Destiny Learning.*

of seven years in the respective building up of physical, etheric, and astral bodies, up to the birth of the ego at age twenty-one. At this point, the life processes are further freed from the body and made available for a new process of learning led by the conscious ego. Adult Learning and Destiny Learning, as they have been developed by Coenraad van Houten, call on us to consciously enhance the life processes for the purpose of learning.

Let us see how the life processes metamorphose in the seven learning processes of Adult Learning (see Table 1). <u>Breathing</u>, in the case of learning, means taking in the external world, everything to which we specifically turn our attention through the senses. The extent to which we can do so can be enhanced by an education of our senses. <u>Warming</u> means adding a qualitative relationship to the given relationship through the senses. It is the warmth of our ego that awakens interest, and forms the intensity of connection essential for learning. In the steps of <u>nourishing</u> and <u>secreting</u>, we take apart what we receive. We examine it, question it, compare it with our own experiences. In brief, this is the analytical part of the process of learning; and it is the part that we are justified in taking from materialistic science.

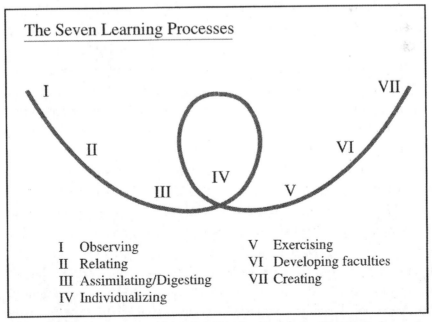

The Seven Learning Processes

I   Observing
II   Relating
III Assimilating/Digesting
IV   Individualizing
V   Exercising
VI   Developing faculties
VII Creating

Table 1: From *Practising Destiny*, Coenraad van Houten, p. 8

However, we need to move further than this step of secreting. This means engaging fully through the forces of our ego with what we have prepared thus far. This is a turning point in which we unite what comes from the outside and make it our own; we individualize it in the fourth step. To get past the external approach of materialistic science, we need to realize that knowledge engages a desire to change inwardly. It puts into motion the forces of will.

The next step is that of maintaining-practicing. In order to sustain change, we need to use rhythm and repetition, through specially devised exercises and activities. We are in fact trying to stimulate new faculties, which is the object of the next phase/life process. To achieve new faculties, we can devise sets of exercises that take into account both the nature of the subject at hand and the inner hindrances that block our learning. The outcome and final stage, reproduction, is reached in the ability to bring forth what has been assimilated and re-elaborated in a purely individual way. We are then able to create something completely new with what we have taken in from the world. The last three life processes are stages of synthesis, and stand as a complement to the scientific/ analytic approach.

The path of Destiny Learning explores our inner being and what approaches us in the events in our lives. Whereas in Adult Learning, we start from what is universal and objective, in Destiny Learning we turn to what is utterly personal and subjective. Ultimately we know that we can reach the objective ground that forms the bedrock of a biography, what we know from spiritual science as our previous incarnations. In that light, we are no longer merely the product of the physical environment and social and cultural forces. We are not only unique manifestations of individuality, but also the result of discernible forces at play in the universe and in our souls. The Mystery Dramas can serve as a blueprint for this perspective. No life in those plays follows the supposedly universal pattern of development, as it is outlined in *Knowledge of Higher Worlds*. Who we are now derives from a higher karmic logic; from who we were in the distant past, from what we set in motion in the present life, and from what others contribute to our personal development. Let us see how that is the case from the perspective of Destiny Learning, as a complementary approach to Adult

Learning (see Table 2). We will look here at Destiny Learning as it is conducted in a workshop lasting three to four days (Destiny Learning Workshop 1). Steps 1 to 4 are part of this process. Steps 5, 6 and 7 (of Destiny Learning Workshops 2 and 3) will be mentioned only briefly.

Once again we start by educating the activity of our senses. We can do that by looking at a significant event in our biography as clearly and objectively as possible. We bring to mind every possible detail of setting, persons, and environment, as well as feelings, sensations, thoughts, and so forth. We "breathe in" the event. In the second step, we place this event in the flow of our biography. In doing this, we recognize it as something that belongs to us, even when it seems to belong to the random caprices of chance. It actually has a place in our biography, and has contributed to shaping us into who we are. In fact, many times the event forms a cluster with other similar events in our lives, and we can recognize a gesture common to all of them. This is why recurring events, rather than the one-of-a-kind, are taken as points of departure for Destiny Learning. The next step is that of digesting; that is, finding the causes and the learning task that emerge from this cluster of events. In

Step	Life Process	Learning to Learn Process	Destiny Learning Process	
I	Breathing	Observing	Observing an event out of life, finding the gesture	
II	Warming	Relating	Placing single event in biography, finding the symptoms of the being	Destiny Learning I
III	Nourishing	Digesting, assimilating	Finding the karmic cause and learning task for this life	
IV	Secreting	Individualizing	Acceptance, saying yes to destiny	
V	Maintaining	Exercising, practising	Practising transformation of your Double	Destiny Learning II
VI	Growing	Growing faculties	Transforming relationships in the network of destiny	
VII	Reproducing	Creating something new	Ordering karma	Destiny Learning III

Table 2: From *The Threefold Nature of Destiny Learning*
C. van Houten, p. 3.

this step we try to reach the deeper, originating causes in a previous life; we wrestle for self-knowledge. This stage is best supported through conversation, art, and exercises, and through the help of a facilitator. In addition to the earlier question ("What are the deeper causes of events in my destiny?") there is another that goes closely in hand with it: "What is this event trying to tell me, and what inner forces do I need to develop in order to integrate it into my life?"

The next stage of individualizing/accepting our destiny pushes us to a step of determination of the will, toward a complete identification with the event. Whereas before I may have looked uncomfortably on the event, or even turned away from it, at this stage this is no longer possible. We now face all the ways in which the double hides from our consciousness, such as in denial or guilt. We can basically recognize the nature, on the one hand, of Luciferic doubles that promote our love of self and estrange us from our real task. On the other hand are the Ahrimanic doubles that harden us and keep us as if imprisoned in the reality of the five senses, in hardbound concepts, and in recurrent patterns of behavior. We are in fact coming to a closer recognition of what lies behind both of them, the "second person in us" who orchestrates the events in our biography.

The next stage of work consists in maintaining/working at transforming our double. Through daily commitment, we learn to recognize the ways through which we limit our freedom in meeting new situations. We can take on the practice of transforming our double in small increments, with what Destiny Learning calls "freer deeds"; actions we may plan carefully, knowing how much we can reasonably expect of ourselves. In fact, initially we could work at transforming the way in which we think of a person with whom we have hostility or difficulties. A next step may be confined to not avoiding him, but greeting him, refraining from commenting at the first sentence, and so forth. In so doing, we may notice how the double reacts in us. At this stage, journaling offers support for observation and knowledge of our inner dynamics, and hence supports the ability to affect the dynamics and transform them.

The next steps move into the abilities that humanity will evolve more fully in the future: developing faculties of karmic perception, and bringing harmony into one's karma. In the first instance we develop the ability to sense from our hearts the forces of destiny. At this stage we have acquired enough familiarity with our double that it gradually takes on the role of guide, letting us know or sense what is possible to carry out in our deeds and what is not yet ripe for action. In the last two stages we can become true agents for social change: first by developing a deeper sense for what a situation calls for, and later by perceiving the deeper links of destiny, and developing the ability to work outside of the karmic ties created from the past (our "Moon karma"). In other words we can truly act freely, and create new "Sun karma."

What may not have clearly emerged from the description given above is the contrasting, yet complementary approach to Adult Learning that Destiny Learning takes. In this context, we will not go into the specifics of how a Destiny Learning workshop or practice is conducted. Suffice it to say that Destiny Learning is assisted through the help of a facilitator and the presence of a group. What counseling and countless peer processes show is that change and emancipation from our shadow/double is a process that requires support and encouragement. We do not change our behavior alone. Many of those who participate in the process of Destiny Learning, through workshops or within ongoing groups, express having a concrete experience of what brotherhood can feel like.

The approach of Destiny Learning contrasts clearly with that of Adult Learning. The second path is mostly an individual path, even when groups can be used for facilitating its steps; that is, study groups. Destiny Learning is indissolubly linked to group activity, given its nature and goals. The education of the will through thinking is accomplished daily in our human environment through the encounters and events that shape our individual destiny. It is not surprising to seek to create learning grounds in a group format—to let the perception of our fellow human beings enrich our own perspective. In thinking we live in the realm of freedom. In the will we live in what conveys the experience of brotherhood.

Reordering our karma lies both in awakening our recollection of previous lives, and in being able to atone for our karmic trespasses and offer soul sacrifice to further the common good. Remembering our karmic past is the deepest and most lasting foundation from which the reordering of karma can follow. What we have said of the Mystery

Dramas holds true in this regard. In fact we could say that Destiny Learning awakens the consciousness of being part of a daily Mystery Drama in which the links of destiny are progressively revealed. The direction of Destiny Learning, its ultimate goal, is the ability to act effectively in the social world; to inwardly know the impact that we can have within our closest circles; and to differentiate between what we can and cannot do.

Gathering All the Strands

We have seen the focus on tolerance and forgiveness in the path described by Prokofieff, and the emphasis on connecting with destiny forces in the approach of Destiny Learning. Yet another approach comes from Harry Salman's and Margreet van den Brink's tentative definition of the "Path of Social Development." They see this way as a complement to the path of schooling that Steiner outlined in *Knowledge of Higher Worlds*. Salman calls it the "heart-path" of the social impulse. He characterizes the two paths as the path to the outer world (the path of thinking) and the path to the inner world (the path of social development). He recognizes the first as the path of choice for the Aristotelian soul, and the second as the path most likely chosen by the Platonic soul. A key aspect he perceives in the second path is the inner growth that results from dialogue and communication. Van den Brink makes this modality concrete in what could be called a "counseling conversation." Finally, van Houten outlines a path that is eminently social through the idea of recognizing that the most deep-rooted difficulties in this life have an origin in previous lives. Most authors see the two paths as complementary to each other. Van den Brink places the social path as a culmination of the individual path. The differences and similarities between the three approaches just explored are summarized in Table 3.

Extending forgiveness, connecting with destiny forces, offering soul sacrifice, atoning, and working at social development are in fact different facets of the same path. Various authors stress different aspects of a larger reality. All of these aspects are present in the "path of the Mystery Dramas." Every aspect of what we have presented above is even more potently present in the legacy of Steiner, to which we are striving to give a name.

Path of Forgiveness (Prokofieff)	Destiny Learning (van Houten	Path of Social Development (van den Brink, Salman)
From tolerance to forgiveness	Learning from life	Dialogue and listening Reliving experiences through the layers of the soul: rational, intellectual and consciousness souls
Moral thinking	Doing 'freer deeds'	Moral path
Spirit self educating the ego	Perceiving our doubles and modifying them over time	Reclaiming awareness of our experiences

Table 3: Path of Forgiveness, Destiny Learning and Path of Social Development

We have seen how Steiner gave his teachings on karma and reincarnation in three subsequent and discontinuous phases. And we have looked at how the understanding of this important theme has evolved ever since Steiner's death. We will now move from looking at phenomena to recognizing the larger archetypes at work behind them.

CHAPTER 4

THE PATH OF SPIRIT RECOLLECTION

What Prokofieff, Salman, Brüll, van den Brink, and van Houten outline from their own research can be carried farther using Steiner's work. To do this, we will turn to an aspect of his legacy that has not received deep attention, partly because it came toward the end of his life, and was not brought to an encompassing organic formulation; that piece is Steiner's "karma exercises." To begin, however, we will first overview a very general principle concerning human interaction: the so-called "archetypal social phenomenon." After taking these two steps, we will move toward a larger characterization of the path of forgiveness, or path of social development, of which van den Brink's counseling conversation or van Houten's Destiny Learning are particular applications.

The Archetypal Social Phenomenon

Toward the last years of his life, particularly from 1918 to 1924, Steiner repeatedly called the attention of members of the Anthroposophical Society to the importance of coming to know oneself in "the encounter," beginning in 1918, when he introduced the idea of the archetypal social phenomenon.

Steiner made clear on more than one occasion that we are truly entering new territory when we tread the social path. "Well, social thinking is different from thinking out of the spirit. In the case of spiritual thinking everything depends on the development of the individuality."[74] There is a dichotomy in the contrast between thinking in the purely cognitive sphere and thinking in the social realm. To underline this dichotomy, Steiner stressed how even those thinkers who significantly contributed to the path of knowledge, Hegel and Fichte, could only offer ideas that were damaging in the social sphere. There is no other way in the social sphere than what individuals work out, from a common interest in each other and a common understanding. Steiner called the earnest interest toward another person the "golden impulse of social life."[75] This is what takes the place of the thinking that has its place in the individual path. In the social path, this encounter and common understanding arise from a deeper understanding of the archetypal social phenomenon.

Let us approach this central phenomenon of the social path; it can be clearly articulated in what happens in a dialogue. Steiner described how when we speak, we put the listener to sleep and awaken to ourselves, and vice versa. We sleep into the other in listening, and awaken to ourselves in speaking. This means that our social impulses are strongest in our sleep, when we are least conscious. "Only that which continues to work out of sleeping into waking conditions is active as a social impulse in ordinary waking consciousness. . . . Thus there exists a permanent disposition to fall asleep precisely in order to build up the social structure of humanity."

The deeper implications of this phenomenon can be gleaned through what Steiner told in the lecture, "The Freeing of Man's Being as the Foundation for a New Social Order."[76] There, Steiner spoke of what happens when we meet our fellow human beings, when we encounter them consciously, and share in the realm of the will. This sharing at the level of the will—understanding what lives in the will of

---

[74] Steiner, *Spiritual Science as a Foundation for Social Forms,* August 29, 1920 lecture.

[75] Steiner, *Christ and the Human Soul,* May 30, 1912 lecture.

[76] Steiner, November 10, 1919 lecture, translated in Baruch Luke Urieli, *Learning to Experience the Etheric World,* 65.

the other—leads us toward a dim reawakening of the bond that exists between two individuals from a preceding incarnation. Naturally this needs to be understood in the right way, and Steiner cautions us, "What manifests itself in this way emerges something like a dream." Once again, this is so because we fall asleep into our fellow human being. However this "dream of repeated earthly lives" is very real. To enhance this understanding of the other, we need to develop our abilities in social life by immersing ourselves lovingly into the other person.

We can now explore the process that is normally working below the threshold of consciousness, as Steiner explores it in his *Philosophy of Freedom*. When I interact with another person, I first of all take in the sensory perceptions at every possible level—sight, hearing, smell, and so forth. All of this sets in motion a train of thought. Through the percept, I move to the formulation of a concept, and realize that this is not likely to be what appears to external senses. Something else is present that the senses cannot immediately reveal. In the act of appearing to my perception, the phenomenon extinguishes itself. This compels the observer to extinguish his own thinking. In fullest consciousness, one would then be able to grasp what thinks in us—the thinking of the other. "The immediate percept, extinguishing itself as a sensory appearance, is grasped by my thinking, and this is a process lying completely below my consciousness, which consists in my thinking being replaced by the other thinking. Through the self-extinguishing of the sensory appearance, the separation between the two spheres of consciousness is actually suspended."[77] This phenomenon mirrors the extinction of consciousness that happens in dreamless sleep. We cannot perceive it because the movement between the extinction and the reawakening of our own consciousness is very rapid; the two states follow one another so quickly that they do not enter our consciousness.

From the description of this phenomenon, we are led to understand that we are truly social when we fall asleep in the other; after that, we need to rescue something from sleeping, and bring it into our waking consciousness. In sleep, in our astral body we find ourselves together

---

[77] Steiner, *Intuitive Thinking as a Spiritual Path: A Philosophy of Freedom*, 1 (Addendum to the Revised Edition of 1918).

with all the other people in our lives, but we are not conscious of it. In the life after death, in kamaloka, we actually awake in the perception of the world of the other person. Social processes are thus "death processes"; hence, they are processes that we normally resist.

In a deep conversation we echo more consciously the processes that occur in the life after death. We come closer to an understanding of the speaker's past, and how his intentions carry him into the future. In effect, we have intimations of his karma, and our own. The speaker fills the listener with his past and future, which are present in the very same intention that draws him to speak. The same is true for the listener as well: his past and future come forward. If we can receive each other in full empathy, we can reach an insight into the person's situation, and the task he or she needs to face. Moreover, the conversation has the ability to awaken the listener to his or her true self. Through compassion, we become especially aware of our own ego. What takes place outside of us also occurs at the same time within us.

The archetypal social phenomenon has a central place in anthroposophic social science. Our social impulses are strongest in our sleep, when we are least conscious. In wanting to stay awake we manifest our antisocial tendencies; and in fact, developing a sense of our true self is the prevalent mission of the present time. This antisocial tendency, even necessity, contributes to illness in our bodies. The social nature in us contributes to our healing; and that cannot be done without going to sleep, to a certain degree.[78] This principle explains, in great measure, why socialization is both one of our time's greatest yearnings, and greatest difficulties.

The assertion of the antisocial impulses will continue for many more centuries; in fact, up until the thirtieth century. We must therefore learn to know others more consciously. This cannot be done through the subconscious, in our feelings. Our current of antipathies and sympathies does not guide us into an understanding of the other any better than our thinking does. In our will, we direct our actions through what we call love, which for the most part is self-love. This self-love is antisocial, and can be transformed only through self-discipline. So, how are we

---

[78] Steiner, *The Challenge of the Times*, December 6, 1918 lecture.

supposed to develop what our natural constitution in the age of the consciousness soul most naturally resists?

To overcome our natural antisocial tendencies in the encounter with others, we must move away from our natural inclination to form concepts about the being of the other, and move toward developing images.[79] Through imaginations, we will acquire a deeper faculty of empathy. Steiner insists that in the future, the social life can be founded only on a development of our imagination. When we meet another person, a picture should arise from the other person. "But this requires of course the heightened interest that I have often described to you as the foundation of social life, in which each person should take in the other person." Here, we must find the social impulses. In fact, Steiner reaches even further, into a description of the sacramental aspect of this type of encounter; he calls it "the capacity to be mystically stimulated" in the encounter with another human being.[80]

Now, the question emerges from reading this last statement of Steiner's: How does Steiner expect that we are to develop this heightened interest, and this capacity of imagining the other human being as objectively as possible? An answer appears in the same lecture, where he spoke of what is now known as the "after-image." To let the after-image reach us,

> It is most important of all that the instinct shall be implanted in people to look back more frequently during this life; but in the right way. To do that, we need to immerse ourselves with real love in the other person. This has such a germinating power over us, that we really acquire the imaginative forces necessary to confront the contemporary human being in such a way that in him, something is manifest that appears to us only after many years in our backward survey of those figures with whom we have lived together.

---

[79] December 6, 1918 lecture.
[80] Ibid, December 7, 1918 lecture.

Notice that what happens naturally after death in kamaloka, is produced in life on earth by the conscious act of will of looking back. Steiner concludes by saying that this is the beginning of real brotherhood. In fact, brotherhood has a place only when we begin to carry the picture of the other person within our soul. This is the kind of elective affinity that replaces the old bonds of blood. We are coming closer to answering the indication we quoted above: "…the instinct shall be implanted in people to look back more frequently during this life, but in the right way." It is obvious that this next step must be more than mere idea or intention.

Steiner looked at two broad ways to reassert the balance between social and antisocial forces. He saw that this could be done externally, as devised through an understanding of social threefolding, and the application of new social forms derived from it; and inwardly, through a repeated effort to awaken the slumbering, unconscious social tendencies. The second option means a conscious working with, and enhancing of, the archetypal social phenomenon; a building of the imaginations that lead to a heightened interest in the other. Social tendencies need to be consciously nurtured through repeated effort. The interest in other human beings can be acquired only through conscious effort; that is why Steiner devised particular exercises.

Bringing the teachings of karma and reincarnation to a concrete understanding in our lives is what Steiner placed at the center of his task. With this, he was intending to counter the natural antisocial tendencies of our times. In future times humanity will hunger for such knowledge and despair at the lack of it. Steiner often pointed to the concrete results he sought through the ideas he bequeathed in his karmic relationships lectures, which were so central to the renewal of the modern Mysteries that was achieved after Christmas of 1923. An example of this intention appears in the lecture of April 16, 1924. "Anthroposophy is not there to develop mere theories of repeated earthly lives, or to give all kinds of schemas, but to show very specific and tangible contexts of life. People will look at the world in a quite different way if we reveal these things… If you know such things, it will become clear that really practical karma reflections are precisely what our civilization needs to give it new impetus and depth."[81]

---

[81] Steiner, *The Roots of Education*, April 16, 1924 lecture.

Steiner's Karma Exercises

To help us be more conscious in our encounters, Steiner formulated many practices and exercises designed for awakening interest, acquiring objectivity, and increasing our understanding of people and events in our lives. In the last twenty-three years of his life, Steiner struggled to bring a living understanding of the ideas of karma and reincarnation. In line with his intention, and central to this attempt, were the exercises that can awaken a sense for individual recognition of the forces of destiny in our biography, and ultimately the reawakening of memories of previous lives. Steiner's effort never received the consecration or ultimate form that the path of thinking finds in *Philosophy of Freedom* or *Knowledge of Higher Worlds*. The reason for this could be that Steiner barely managed to complete laying out important blocks of this edifice in the last year of his life. Nevertheless, a whole, coherent direction emerges once we look at some of these exercises, arranging them from the most immediate to the most demanding. This review is in no way exhaustive; it is merely indicative of the breadth of Steiner's work in the matter. Some of the names chosen for nine of these exercises are the author's choice.

Karma Exercise I: Gratitude Recollection

A first exercise that forms a prelude to the series that we will examine is designed to awaken gratitude and a sense of perspective concerning our personal achievements.[82] In it, Steiner asks us to turn back to an overview of our life and see what part other people have played in it, by detecting how much we owe to our parents, relatives, friends, teachers, colleagues, and so forth. The exercise should lead to the realization of how much in our life we owe to others. Repeated over time, it allows us to develop an imagination for those people who play an important part in our life, an imagination that points to their deeper being. A variation on this exercise is offered in the lecture "Social and Anti-Social Forces in the Human Being," and goes a step further.[83] We are asked to bring

---

[82] Steiner, *Inner Aspect of the Social Question*, February 4, 1919 lecture.
[83] Steiner, "Social and Anti-social Forces in the Human Being," December 6, 1918 lecture.

before our mind's eye images of those who have played a role in our lives, either directly and positively, or indirectly through hindrance and opposition, and see them as vividly as possible. We should be able to develop an objective sense of our indebtedness. Steiner has this gripping comment to offer: "It is extremely important, for the ability to inwardly picture another individual without love or hate, to give space to another individual within our souls, as it were; this is a faculty which is diminishing week by week in the evolution of humanity. It is a capacity which we are losing completely, by degrees; we pass one another by without arousing the slightest mutual interest." By invigorating this ability, we develop a truer picture of the people in our lives, in effect, an imagination of them. This will develop further in the ability to "relate ourselves imaginatively to those we meet in the present."

Karma Exercise II: Phase of Life Recollection

An exercise that anticipates the so-called Lesser Karma Exercise is the one Steiner described in the same lecture quoted above as a complement to the first. Whereas in the exercise above, we are seeking to develop an objective and imaginative perception of others, here the same is true about ourselves. In this instance, we will refer to a particular stage of our lives, and immerse ourselves objectively into that time, as if we were spectators of ourselves. In so doing, we are freeing the perception of ourselves in the present from the images that bind us to the past, and that lead us to identify our ego with our life experiences, rather than with the intimations of our higher self. We thus develop an imaginative picture of ourselves, and lessen the effects of the egoism that naturally develops in our age of the consciousness soul. None of this can be achieved without repeated effort. "According to true occult science, nothing can be done by remaining in place, for one forgets things and must always be cultivating them afresh. This is just as it should be, for fresh efforts need to be continually made."

Karma Exercise III: Basic Lesser Karma Exercise

A next simple exercise, the "Lesser Karma Exercise," consists of looking back to one single event in our life, one that is seemingly due to chance, or to something that we did not wish to happen. Steiner spoke of this exercise in more than one place.[84]

The example that Steiner offers is that of a shingle falling from a roof onto our head. He asks us to imagine the deed of the "second person in us" who loosens the shingle from the roof just in time for it to fall on our heads when we pass under it. In other words, he wants us to picture that we have planned our lives before our birth in such a way as to come to certain critical turning points on earth. When we enter the exercise for the first few times, this second man is clearly seen as an invention, something artificially conjured up. However, he grows and evolves in us to the point that we cannot escape the feeling that he really is within us, accompanied with the growing realization that we have really wanted these events to come to pass. The memory of the fact that we have wanted these events has been all but erased from our consciousness; and the exercise, repeated over many life events, serves to awaken it. We can thus deepen an inner conviction and feeling for our karmic biography. Cultivating this feeling bestows deep inner strength, and modifies our attitude toward events we may have previously confronted with fear. We acquire a certain peacefulness and acceptance, together with the feeling that everything in our life has a purpose. This can even go further, as Steiner points to in a lecture of 1912.[85] "Through such mental pictures—that we ourselves have willed the chance events in our life—we arouse, in the life of feeling, memory of our earlier incarnations. In this way we understand that we are rooted in the spiritual world, we begin to understand our destiny." Whether or not we attain more than a simple feeling for the tenor of our past lives, something else becomes apparent: we start taking responsibility for our destiny, and stop blaming parents, friends, enemies, or random events for those things that cause us unhappiness.

---

[84] Steiner, *Karma and Reincarnation*, January 30, 1912 lecture. See also: January 29, 1912 and February 8, 1912 lectures in *Esoteric Christianity and the Mission of Christian Rosenkreutz*.

[85] Steiner, *Esoteric Christianity*, January 29, 1912 lecture.

Karma Exercise IV: Attitude Toward Joy and Happiness

When the previous exercise has become an ingrained practice or changed our inner disposition, our attitude towards joy and happiness will change, although this step may not be easy. One will come through joy and happiness to feelings of thorough shame. And the only way to rid oneself of these feelings is to realize that we have not earned this happiness. "This is the only cure, for otherwise the shame may be so intense that it almost shatters the soul. The only salvation is not to attribute our joys to the wiser being within us." And doing this will allow the feeling of shame to pass. In its place comes a new feeling of peaceful security in the spirit, and thankfulness towards the guiding powers of humanity. "If [the human being] ascribes joy and happiness to his karma he is succumbing to a fallacy which weakens and paralyses the spiritual within him."[86]

Karma Exercise V: "Contrary Being" Exercise

The Lesser Karma Exercise is developed to the extreme in the exercise that Steiner offered in the lecture of January 23, 1912.[87] In this exercise, we are asked to have a retrospective look at our life, and see our propensities, both for what comes naturally and what does not. We are asked to focus mostly on what we could not develop; on what became of us in spite of our desires to the contrary; on everything that we wanted to flee from, and have not managed to escape. When that image of this "contrary" being has been carefully built up, we are asked to immerse ourselves in this being, and completely identify with it. From this exercise, we will derive some level of understanding for something that does not come from this life but from previous incarnations. In this instance, we are no longer looking at a separate undesired event in our life, but at the sum total of all undesired events, as a whole gesture within our being.

---

[86] Steiner, *Esoteric Christianity*, February 8, 1912 lecture.
[87] Steiner, *Karma and Reincarnation*.

Karma Exercise VI: Grace Events Recollection

An exercise that is somehow the reverse of the Lesser Karma Exercise consists in consciously looking back at what did not happen, at what we were spared. The graphic example consists of looking at what held us back, pausing to look at a flower or at the landscape; seconds later, a boulder detached from the cliff above and fell, passing a few yards ahead of us, thereby avoiding us. In a less dramatic manner, there are countless encounters that would not have happened in our lives were it not for delays, changes of plans, or last-minute decisions. Observing these events leads us to break away from a strictly mechanistic cause-and-effect mentality, and to develop an ability to perceive the chain of events that constantly unfolds in front of our eyes by virtue of the forces of karma.

Karma Exercise VII: Extended Lesser Karma Exercise

An enhancement of the Lesser Karma Exercise appears in *Secrets of the Threshold*.[88] There Steiner asks us to go back over our last three or four weeks; or better, the last three to four months. We look at everything that has taken place in this period of time. In doing this, we lay aside the idea that any undesired event was the result of an injustice caused to us. Likewise we lay aside any self-justifications we could invoke for our shortcomings. In brief, we place all responsibility for our life at our own feet. This exercise awakens us to a new relationship with the spiritual world; that is, a relationship with the "second person in us" who arranges the events in our lives. We will continue this series with two exercises specifically designed for the perception of previous lives; both of them were given to us by Steiner in 1924.

---

[88] Steiner, *Secrets of the Threshold*, August 31, 1913 lecture.

Karma Exercise VIII: Moon/ Saturn/ Sun Exercise

The first could be called the "Moon/ Saturn/ Sun Exercise."[89] This can be applied to another person or to oneself. Here it is a matter of peeling layers of the personality; of seeing more and more deeply into the real human nature, rather than what our senses present us of the human being, by looking at the threefoldness of willing, feeling, and thinking. In meditation we first look at the person by disregarding everything that he achieves in life by virtue of what he can accomplish through his arms and legs, disregarding where he goes, where he lived, what he does professionally, how he moves. One focuses instead on temperament, mood, way of thinking, and so forth. It is a way to render the man transparent to everything that works in his will. Behind the picture of the individual thus elaborated starts to shine the spiritual Moon; that is, everything that works from the Moon sphere upon the person.

In the next stage, we further disregard what comes from his life of emotions, from the temperament, everything of a soul nature; and further, also disregard what the man receives through his senses. All that is left is the way the person thinks. At this point, the whole of the rhythmic system has been rendered transparent, and behind shines what comes through the spiritual Sun.

In the final stage, we also disregard what comes from the person's thinking, in order to behold what shines behind the man; he is thus made wholly "transparent," and one beholds the impulses shining from Saturn. At that moment, one can start seeing the individual as a spiritual being, and start perceiving his karma.

Karma Exercise IX: Greater Karma Exercise

A final exercise is the so-called four days/ three nights exercise or the "Greater Karma Exercise."[90] Here it is a matter of bringing back to memory an event from daily life that may or may not involve another

---

[89] Steiner, *Karmic Relationships*, Volume 2 (London: Rudolf Steiner Press, 1997) May 4, 1924 lecture.
[90] Ibid, May 9, 1924 lecture.

person. It is a matter of depicting it inwardly, or "painting it spiritually," as Steiner puts it, by recreating in greatest detail all the impressions received by our senses. If the memory includes a person, one re-creates inwardly the way in which she moved; the quality, pitch, and tone of her voice; words used, gestures, smells, and so forth. This experience is taken into the night and repeated the following two days. The image is first given shape by the astral body in the external ether. From there, the next morning the image is impressed into the etheric body. One awakens with definite feelings and the impression that the image wants something from us. It grows real in us. The etheric body continues to work on the image. On the third day, the image is impressed into the physical body. There the image is spiritualized. Steiner describes the experience of the day as a cloud in which the person moves. It gives rise to the feeling of being part of the picture itself. At first we feel part of the picture, but with our will paralyzed, frozen, so to speak. This experience then evolves and becomes sight, an objective image. This will be the image of the event of the previous life that was the root cause of the event in the present incarnation. An experience of this kind will most likely not arise until the exercise is carried out a great number of times.

Before moving further, we can look at the contrast between Lesser and Greater Karma Exercises. The distinction is significant. The first stage is one of "taking responsibility for our lives"; the second leads to precise knowledge. The first stage is emblematically reached by the character of Strader in *The Souls' Awakening* with the words "And yet will come what has to come about" ["And yet … what must be *will* be."] (Scene 1, Ruth and Hans Pusch translation). Strader has acquired an unshakeable faith in the wise guidance of karma, one that leads him to accept bitter opposition, and even complete paralysis in his life pursuits, with the knowledge that other doors will open to him after death. Quite differently from him, Thomasius encounters tremendous challenges with an aspect of his double, called "the spirit of Johannes' Youth," and only manages to dispel this being through knowledge of his previous incarnation as an Egyptian woman (*Souls' Awakening*, Scene 10). This second instance illustrates a stage that can be attained through the Greater Karma Exercise.

Exercises I-II	Exercises III to VII	Exercises VIII and IX
Seeing Ourselves as a Stranger	Lesser karma exercise	Greater karma exercise
Developing imaginative pictures of self and others	Taking responsibility for our lives.	Perceiving the causes in previous life events.

Table 4: Exercises of Spirit Recollection

We can graphically present the evolution of Steiner's exercises of Spirit Recollection in Table 4. All of these imply a strengthening of our powers of observation, and of our memory. The quintessential exercise that forms the foundation and prelude for all of them is the rückschau. The activity of the rückschau is one of pure review, deprived of evaluation. As we move towards the other exercises, review is mixed with as objective as possible an evaluation element. Only the rückschau is pure observation and memory.

A Review of the Karmic Exercises

Deciding to work with forces of destiny entails at first great effort of education of the will (usually resisted by our soul) to reconnect with our pre-birth resolves. Before incarnating, we were offered a preview of the challenges to come, and we accepted them with joy and earnestness, in order to advance our karma and the karma of those we love. A veil of forgetfulness was drawn over this experience for our lives on earth, and we have to struggle long and hard to recapture knowledge of our pre-birth intentions; such knowledge, however, enlivens meaning in our lives. The Lesser Karma Exercise and its variations reconnect us with our pre-birth intentions. The exercises are also a means to anticipate what normally occurs after death, in the kamaloka condition. Taking responsibility means being willing to live in the consequences of our actions, in their full ramifications; hence, it also means being willing to experience how these actions have affected other human beings.

A deeper level of resolve was attained at the so-called Cosmic

Midnight. This is an experience that we cannot always undergo in full consciousness. It is during the Cosmic Midnight that we behold the full dimension of our humanity. Recollection of our previous lives forms an important part of this experience, as we saw in the *Mystery Dramas*. It is this deeper level that leads us to the objective knowledge that the Greater Karma Exercise addresses. The distinction between the Lesser and Greater Karma Exercises also matches Prokofieff's assertion that it is not necessary to know about anthroposophy in the first stages of the path of forgiveness up to the Lesser Karma Exercise. Exertion of the will, through repeated practice of exercises or deeds that we do not naturally feel inclined to accomplish, forms the foundation for this path. Deeper spiritual knowledge, however, becomes necessary once we want to move deeper, to the root causes of events in our biography in previous lives.

It is important to mention that the above list is not exhaustive and that there are other exercises that complement the ones mentioned above.[91] Finally, the overview would not be complete without the two "exercises" that Steiner mentioned in *Karmic Relationships*, Volume 3,

---

[91] A particular kind of exercises consists in what Steiner calls "looking for ourselves in the world." They are found in the lecture of March 5, 1918 in *Earthly Death and Cosmic Life* (London: Rudolf Steiner Press, 1964), March 5, 1918 lecture. These exercises are mentioned in relation to finding our connection with the departed souls.

The first exercise consists in reflecting on all that has come to pass by virtue of what we were prevented from doing. An example of it is that of a man accustomed to taking a regular walk. At one point in his walk an urgent inner impulse drove him to stop just before a boulder fell from a cliff. The impulse to stop prevented the boulder from crushing him. Similar, much less dramatic events happen with regularity in our lives. We usually seek for an understanding between what happened before and what occurred afterwards, but we seldom stop to look at what would have happened had things happened as originally intended; in other words, what did not happen. This leads Steiner to say "... seeking the connection of what follows with what has gone before is a very one-sided way of looking at life." With this newer perspective "we come to see ourselves so to speak, in the midst of our environment, and we see how it forms us and leads us forward incrementally." Steiner is encouraging us to an environmental listening of what the future calls into being, if we are just able to see and sense how we are continuously inserted in a larger weaving of threads of karma. In this weaving the future that wants to come into being has as much importance as the past.

and that he repeatedly asked of members: researching whether we are Aristotelian or Platonic souls; and whether we are Old or Young Souls. Knowing which stream we belong to expands the concept of Spirit Recollection from an individual to a collective/historical perspective, and places us at the beginning of the path of karmic research.

Karmic Research

When Steiner offered us his practical karma exercises, he had abundantly put them to the test; he was thus able to follow the evolution, the "becoming," of many personalities over the centuries. We can see in those concrete examples what Steiner meant by "developing imaginations of other human beings." We can also see how these imaginations can serve as the antidote to the loss of interest in each other that humanity faces as a serious danger, more and more, as time goes by. It was through a heightened interest, and the capacity to develop imaginations about each individual, that Steiner could enter into a lively intercourse with the "I" of the individuals he wanted to know. Eduard von Hartmann and Fercher von Steinwand are examples of some of the earliest individuals

---

A second exercise consists in looking at the impulses of will from which we operate which are most of the time below the threshold of consciousness, "an underground thought at the basis of our life that does not enter our ordinary lives." One such instance is the "thought that drives us out of bed." Do we get up because we hear the pot of coffee brewing? Do we awake because worries crowd our mind? Or is it the thought of whom we are going to meet during the day? And this observation needs to be carried out over a number of days. Doing this simply allows us to raise into consciousness the "underground thoughts" that lie below consciousness.

A third exercise, variation of the previous one, consists in becoming aware of the effect our presence has on an environment. How does a room with other individuals get affected by our presence, e.g. in the moment in which we enter or in the moment in which we leave? Steiner offers two contrasting examples. The first is that individual who glides in and out without causing much notice "as if an angel had flitted in and out." A second person may have such a strong presence that it may seem he came "with all sorts of invisible feet." This exercise serves to awaken a "sensitivity to karma" by allowing us to see in the environment a reflection of our own being.

whose "I" Steiner could keenly sense. We can look with deeper insight at the example of von Hartmann, as one of many, because here Steiner tells us what made it possible to break through to a beholding of his previous incarnations. The turning point lay not in the philosopher's prodigious amount of writing, nor in its content. Rather, Steiner looked at the fact that before becoming a philosopher, von Hartmann had been a military officer interested in his task and in sword-fighting; but he was not prone to mental speculation. Then an illness caused him an incapacity in the knee, which persisted the rest of his life, and caused his discharge from the army on a pension. After that, Hartmann the philosopher was born. Steiner had put his finger on his very unusual way to come to philosophy; from there, Steiner traced Hartmann's incarnations back to a "remarkably clever and able individuality in very ancient times"; and later to a Crusader who suffered a sunstroke that caused an inability to think. The loss of ability to think was the result of a wrong, committed through cleverness in the previous incarnation. As a Crusader, von Hartmann had fought against the Turks and other Asiatic people, but in the process he acquired tremendous admiration for their civilization.[92]

Equally revealing is everything that Steiner offered about Frank Wedekind in his *Autobiography*. These are some of his observations:

> What hands! In a previous lifetime they must have accomplished things possible only for one who can allow the force of spirit to flow into the finest divergence of the fingers. ... And his expressive head—as though shaped completely by this exceptional quality of will in his hands. ... But gestures of his arms in response to the sensitivity of those hands showed that he was more likely to withdraw from the world—a spirit who placed himself beyond the hustle and bustle of modern humanity, but was unable to be clear about what past age he belonged to.[93]

---

[92] Steiner, *Karmic Relationships*, Volume 1, March 15, 1924 lecture.
[93] Steiner, *Autobiography*, Chapter 55.

What an incredible characterization emerges from just these few lines! Other indications of this individuality come from one of Steiner's *Karmic Relationships* lectures.[94] Frank Wedekind had been a pupil of the great alchemist Basilius Valentinus. However, his alchemical work had not been properly coordinated with the corresponding sense activity. This led him, in the later incarnation of the dramatist, to observe facts and string them together in a way that Steiner called "often repellent," rendering his dramas far from common, as well as hard to understand, but not in the least philistine.

Steiner's loving attention to the details of a biography, such as one's body or soul gestures, allowed him to create an imagination of numerous individuals, sometimes after great efforts. Keen interest, and ability to discern the details that matter (those that make the individual unique) are the starting point into karma research. This is an important aspect of what Steiner developed from the heart of his mission. What is Goethean observation in the natural realm, becomes here an interest-filled beholding of the unique characteristics of the other person that leaves no place for sympathy or antipathy.

---

[94] Steiner, *Karmic Relationships*, Volume 2, April 26, 1924 lecture.

CHAPTER 5

THE PATH OF SPIRIT RECOLLECTION IN RELATION TO SPIRIT BEHOLDING

We have reviewed the exercises through which Steiner offers us tools for awakening the perception of the forces of karma. We can now try to find some guidelines and commonalities among all of the exercises. In the first series of exercises, we try to recapture an event in time, or move back in time to a few weeks or few months earlier, or even view the whole of our life (Gratitude Recollection). Through the Lesser Karma Exercise, emphasis is laid on the idea that the second man in us, our higher self, is meeting us even in those events that we tend to attribute to random chance, or that we blame on fate or on others. We are gently led to adopt the reverse stance to what is most habitual for people who do not take the reality of karma and reincarnation to heart. In the exercises that are most meditative (The Moon/ Sun/ Saturn Exercise and the Greater Karma Exercise), we then move recollection to its extremes, to the primal cause of our karma, to our previous lives. All of the abovementioned exercises form an extension of the rückschau, which is a basic archetypal exercise for going back over the events of the day in reverse order. In the rückschau, we focus on the purely factual, leaving aside anything that may be of a feeling nature, or of a will-evaluation nature.

What the rückschau and all of the other exercises described have in common is the idea of looking back to the essence of our "being in time." What psychology sees as causes in our early childhood and upbringing, spiritual science seeks in the apprehension of our previous lives. We ourselves are the primary cause, not our environment. This is why letting go of blame, assuming responsibility, and developing empathy and self-empathy are fruitful preliminary exercises, before attempting to retrieve memories of previous lives. These practices allow us to become familiar with the notion that we bear the primary responsibility for our destiny.

In the exercises described, we have retraced much of what is outlined in the four *Mystery Dramas*, from *The Portal of Initiation* to *The Soul's Awakening*. The whole of Steiner's intention behind the spreading of the teachings of karma, the writing of the *Mystery Dramas*, and the assignment of exercises and practices finds its expression in the human being's ability to follow the path of "Spirit Recollection" or "Spirit Recalling" that resounds in the words of the Foundation Stone Meditation. In an excerpt from the first panel (or verse) of the meditation we hear:

> Soul of Man!
> Thou livest in the limbs
> Which bear you through the world of space
> Into the ocean-being of the spirit.
> Practice spirit-recollection
> In the depths of soul,
> Where in the wielding
> World-Creator-Life
> Thine Own Being
> Comes to being
> Within the I of God
> Then in the All-World-Being of Man
> Thou will truly live.
>
> For the Father-Spirit of the heights holds sway
> In Depths of worlds, begetting life.
> Seraphim, Cherubim, Thrones!

Let there ring out from the Heights
What in the Depths is echoed,
Speaking:
Ex Deo nascimur.
The Elemental Beings hear it
In East and West and North and South:
May human beings hear it!

These sentences indicate that through the path of Spirit Recollection we can, ideally, endeavor to retrace our steps toward the time in which incarnation first began, to the Lemurian Epoch, the time before which our "own being comes to being within God's I" ("Ex Deo nascimur"). This is why "Spirit Recollection" is the term I will adopt for describing an overarching impulse; the path of forgiveness and the path of social development are particular manifestations or characterizations of this impulse. The counseling conversation and Destiny Learning are particular techniques for acquiring the skills of spirit recollection.

We can now explore the same theme from the polarity of paths that Steiner introduced in 1923, which complement what has been said so far, and allow us to look further into the contrast between Spirit Recollection and Spirit Beholding (also called Spirit Vision).

Saturn and Moon Paths

Let us bring this line of research to a conclusion. We will examine some characterizations that were expressed by Steiner after the Christmas Conference. In the lecture of February 6, 1923, we are introduced to the contrast between the "path of Saturn" and the "path of the Moon."[95]

To refer to the Saturn path, or path of thinking, Steiner took his start from the *Philosophy of Freedom*. There he described the process through which thinking is resurrected from a passive activity (abstract thinking), into a path of perception of the spiritual, when the thinker tries to apprehend the relationship between thinking and himself (which Steiner characterized as pure thinking). Steiner described "how the will strikes

---

[95] Steiner, *Awakening to Community*, February 6, 1923 lecture.

into the otherwise passive realm of thought, stirring it awake and making the thinker inwardly active." This is the path that takes the human being beyond Saturn into the universe (the path to the macrocosm). Steiner continued, "in that book [*Philosophy of Freedom*] I limited the discussion entirely to the world of the senses, keeping more advanced aspects for later works, because matters like these have to be gradually developed."

The first path (Saturn, pure thinking) is then contrasted with the Moon path, the one in which "one can advance on the opposite side [microcosm] by entering deeply into the will, to the extent of becoming wholly quiescent, by becoming a pole of stillness in the motion one otherwise engenders in the will." Instead of becoming an unconscious part of world movement, one can consciously come to a standstill. Through this "one succeeds in keeping the soul still while the body moves through space; succeeds in being active in the world while the soul remains quiet; carries activity, and at the same time quietly observes it; then thinking suffuses the will, just as the will previously suffused thinking." This second path (Moon path) is what allows one to separate the will from the physical body. "One learns to say 'You harbor in your will sphere a great variety of drives, instincts and passions. But . . . they belong to a different world that merely extends into this one, a world that keeps its activity quite separate from everything that has to do with the sense world.'"

From the explorations of this chapter and the previous we can now recapitulate the findings. In the lecture quoted above, Steiner described the two paths of inner development; then he said, "I am only giving you a sketch of these matters today, because I want to characterize the third phase of anthroposophy." By "third phase," he meant the historical phase, in which more and more individuals working out of anthroposophy carried the deepest yearning to undertake projects in the world; the period in which anthroposophy gave rise to various practical applications. It is characteristic that Steiner prefaced the outline of the two paths in the same lecture, thus: "In view of the deliberations that have been going on here with the reorganization of the Anthroposophical Society [and the forming of the Free Anthroposophical Society] as their object, I would like to shape today's lecture in a way that may help my hearers form independent judgments in these decisive days." This shows that the different orientation towards the Saturn or the Moon path had a great deal to do with the difficulties between the older and younger generations. It was important for Steiner to offer a bridge for mutual understanding of the two tendencies.

Spirit Recollection and Spirit Beholding

New key elements about the contrast mentioned above could be added only after the Christmas Conference. What Steiner characterized only in a sketch is deepened in various stages, in his *Leading Thoughts*.[96] We will turn first to *Leading Thoughts* 95 to 99, quoting extensively from them, and then to Letter 17 of July 13, 1924, "Understanding of the Spirit and Conscious Experience of Destiny."

Leading Thought 95 (September 21, 1924) expresses: "In the manifestation of the Will, Karma works itself out. But its working remains in the unconscious. By lifting to conscious imagination what works unconsciously in the Will, Karma is apprehended. Man feels his destiny within him."

Leading Thoughts 98 and 99 (September 28, 1924) reiterate these notions by further expressing the key difference between karma from the past and future karma: "The Feeling and Willing of Thought contain the karmic outcome of past lives on Earth. The Thinking and Willing of the life of Feeling karmically determine man's character. The Thinking and Feeling of the life of Will tear the present earthly life away from Karmic connections." (LT 98) And further: "In the Feeling and Willing of Thinking man lives out his Karma of the past; in the Thinking and Feeling of Willing he prepares the Karma of the future." (LT 99)

The above premises find a culmination in Letter 17 of July 6, 1924, "Understanding of the Spirit and Conscious Experience of Destiny" (see Appendix 2). Here Steiner contrasts again the two paths—previously defined as Saturn (cognitive) and Moon (will) paths. The first path is such that the human being can think, "I am forming thoughts about what my senses reveal to me as the world," and he can experience

---

[96] Steiner, *Anthroposophical Leading Thoughts: Anthroposophy as a Path of Knowledge; The Michael Mystery.*

himself in his thinking, and therefore become conscious of the self. In the path of the will one directs one's own attention to the inner world; then those events emerge into consciousness that belong to our life's destiny, and in which our human self has flowed along from the point of time in which our memory goes back. In following up the events of his destiny, a man experiences his own existence. The human being who experiences this enhanced memory can tell himself, "I with my own self have experienced something that destiny brought to me." This modality in the second path awakens the consciousness that one is not alone in one's destiny, and that the world enters into the expression of one's will. Therefore one goes from experiencing oneself to experiencing the world.

To recapitulate the contrast, through experiencing the world in thinking one can experience oneself; through going the path of the soul, one can experience the world. The one who takes the latter path, therefore, does not lose himself in the world of his own soul, as he would in false mysticism; he can receive a feeling of communion with the world even from the starting point of his own experience. Finally, this path means acquiring the feeling of receiving one's "I" from the world. And Steiner concludes, "Anthroposophy finds the self by showing how the sense-world reveals to man not only sense perceptions, but also the after-effects of his life before birth and his former earthly lives."

From the extensive quotations given above, we can detect that in the space of one year alone, from 1923 to 1924, Steiner moved from a general to a much deeper characterization of the path of the will (through thinking). This change was made fully possible by the background offered through the teachings of karma and reincarnation after the Christmas Conference.

The contrast between Spirit Recollection and Spirit Beholding is completed in the encompassing expression of the Foundation Stone Meditation. We have looked at the first verse, or panel, in relation to the path of Spirit Recollection. We will now look at what is said in relation to the third panel and Spirit Beholding. Let us keep in mind that the imagination of the mantram needs the balance brought in by the second panel, which is the only one that mentions the Christ. We will return later to this in the next chapter. In the third panel we are told:

Soul of Man!
Thou livest in the resting Head
Which from the ground of the Eternal
Opens to the the thoughts of Worlds.
Practice Spirit-Vision
In quietness of Thought,
Where the eternal aims of Gods
World-Being's Light
On thine own I
Bestow
For thy free Willing.
Then from the grounds of the Spirit of man
Thou will truly think

For the Spirit's Universal Thoughts hold sway
In the Being of all world, beseeching Light.
Archai, Archangeloi, Angeloi!
Let there be prayed in the Depths
What from the Heights is answered,
Speaking:
Per Spiritum Sanctum reviviscimus.
The Elemental Beings hear it
In East and West and North and South
May human beings hear it!

Here, it could not be clearer that it is through thinking that we can apprehend the working of the spirit, in the quiet of the head. And thinking, penetrated through and through by the will, is what allows us to truly think "in grounds of the Spirit in Man." In contrast, the first panel indicates that Spirit Recollection allows us "to truly live…in the All-World-Being of Man."

It is very indicative that Steiner made repeated references to the contrast of the two paths in the years 1923 to 1924. All that has been brought forward above appears succinctly restated in the letter to all members, July 13, 1924 ("Understanding of the Spirit and Conscious Experience of Destiny"). The entire letter is given in Appendix 1.

The path of Spirit Beholding is the path of thinking transformed by the will. The path of Spirit Recollection is the path in which the will is transformed through thinking. This transformation is made possible by recollection, the activity that consists in looking back, both in reviewing factually, and in evaluating morally.

On the path of knowledge, the exercises in *Knowledge of Higher Worlds*, meditation, and the whole of anthroposophy form the essential foundation, which accompanies the pupil in his higher understanding of how the spirit permeates everything that we behold through the senses. To this, the Six Basic Exercises are added as an important complement.

In Spirit Recollection, the exercises we have described and other similar ones, form the essential core of the path. The whole of anthroposophy and even knowledge of karma and reincarnation (as important as they may be) form the complement. In fact, to walk at least the first stages on the path of the will, as Prokofieff confirms, it is not necessary to know anthroposophy. And the attitude of soul necessary on this second path also differs greatly from the Saturn path. This difference is clearly stated in *Philosophy of Freedom's* Chapter 12, "Moral Imagination." In contrasting natural-scientific knowledge (and all external knowledge) with knowledge that leads to moral action, Steiner said:

> The confusion arises because, as natural scientists, we already have the facts before us and afterwards investigate them cognitively; while for ethical action, we must ourselves first create the facts that we cognize afterward. In the evolutionary process of the world order, we accomplish something that, on a lower level, is accomplished by nature: we alter something perceptible. Thus, initially, the ethical norm cannot be cognized like a natural law; rather, it must be created. Only once it is present can it become the object of cognition.

The contrast between the two paths appears emblematically when we look at the polarities between the "pencil exercise" and the rückschau, as expressions of Spirit Beholding and Spirit Recollection respectively.

In the pencil exercise we focus all our attention on an object, such as a pencil, by discerning our sense impressions of the object, thinking about its component parts and their relationships, imagining the steps of the process that created it, etc. During the few minutes of the observation all thoughts foreign to the object are carefully kept at bay, and that requires a tremendous effort of the will. It is truly an education of thinking through the will. The polarity, though not immediately apparent, is realized in the rückschau exercise. The intent is to focus inwardly upon the whole of the day or parts of it, picturing the events in the reverse order of their occurrence, and even in reverse motion. Instead of looking outwardly, we turn our focus inwardly with an effort of our memory. What our will has brought about throughout the day, all of which would remain unconscious or semi-conscious, is raised to awareness. This is also a conscious effort of the will, but here thinking places order in the unfolding of the will which was previously brought about during the day, reminding us of what Steiner tells us is the precondition for ethical action in which "we must ourselves first create the facts." Looking outwardly in the pencil exercise becomes looking inwardly in the rückschau; the first addresses the thinking through the will, the second the will through thinking.

The conclusions reached through this study are echoed by Zeylmans van Emmichoven, who dedicated his life to the understanding of the Christmas Conference and of the Foundation Stone Meditation. Here is his contrast between Spirit Recollection and Spirit Beholding: "'Practice spirit remembering' not only means that we learn how our own 'I' is part of God's 'I'—no, out of cosmic heights we hear resound: 'From the divine, humanity takes its existence,' the humanity together with which we must come to a brotherly, social community. ... The third task set us, 'Practice spirit vision,' is ultimately the path from natural science to spiritual science, from anthropology to anthroposophy." We will return to what van Emmichoven describes as Spirit Mindfulness by the end of the next chapter.[97] Of added interest is what he says, very

---

[97] Emanuel Zeylmans, *Willem Zeylmans von Emmichoven: An Inspiration for Anthroposophy. A biography*, 249.

briefly and specifically, about the path of Spirit Beholding in his book *The Foundation Stone*.[98]

In *The Occult Significance of Forgiveness*, Prokofieff offers examples of individuals who practice the "path of forgiveness" without any knowledge of anthroposophy.[99] The path of forgiveness is a particular formulation of the larger path of Spirit Recollection. Abundant evidence of the same is offered in *A Revolution of Hope*[100], Chapter 6, where I described various moral techniques that have emerged in the twentieth century: the Twelve Step program, Hellinger's Family Constellations, Nonviolent Communication, Appreciative Inquiry, World Café, Future Search, Theory U, Peacemaking Circles, and so forth. Many others could be named, such as the field of Life-Coaching, Playback Theater, Dynamic Facilitation, Technology of Participation, etc. These techniques cover the first stages of the path of Spirit Recollection up to the Lesser Karma Exercise. No previous cognitive background is necessary in order to work with these approaches. Certainly anthroposophy adds strength to those who engage in the path of the will, and anthroposophic knowledge becomes essential in the later stages of the path of Spirit Recollection, which in effect leads us to a personal understanding of the laws of karma and reincarnation. Table 5 summarizes the contrast between the paths of Spirit Recollection and Spirit Beholding.

We have characterized a path fully distinct from the path of knowledge in the narrower sense, that of Spirit Beholding. The formulation of this contrast clearly appeared only at the end of Steiner's life. However, we can also retrace the complementarity of the two paths in Steiner's earlier work. Although he focused primarily on the path of knowledge, or Spirit Beholding, the path of Spirit Recollection played a subsidiary role. That is the place of some of the Six Basic or Subsidiary Exercises (except control of thought), next to the specific exercises that form the essence of *Knowledge of Higher Worlds*. The Six Basic Exercises were introduced in *Occult Science* (Chapter 5, "Cognition of the Higher Worlds: Initiation"). These are: control of thought, control of feeling,

---

[98] F. Willem, Zeylmans van Emmichoven, *The Foundation Stone*, 42-43.
[99] Prokofieff, *Occult Significance of Forgiveness*, Chapter 3.
[100] Morelli, *A Revolution of Hope: Spirituality, Cultural Renewal and Social Change*.

control of the will, positivity, open-mindedness, and harmonious overall integration of the previous five. Among the aims of the exercises is this stated goal as a preparation for spiritual training: "Whoever, in this way, endeavors to regulate his soul life will also attain the possibility of self-observation, through which he observes his own affairs with the same tranquility as if they were those of others," in effect very reminiscent of what has been said of the Moon path or of the exercises of Spirit Recollection. It is in the context of *Occult Science* that Steiner also introduced the rückschau, an exercise to review the day in reverse order, from end to beginning. Similar to the Six Exercises are the "seven requirements" expressed in Chapter 5, "Requirements for Esoteric Training," in *Knowledge of Higher Worlds*. These are: improvement of

SPIRIT BEHOLDING	SPIRIT RECOLLECTION
Saturn path (macrocosm)	Moon Path (microcosm)
Path of thinking through the will	Path of the will through thinking
Pencil observation exercise: looking at the outer world	Rückschau: looking at the inner world
Preparation through study of anthroposophy	Preparation through the karma exercises: review exercises going first to lesser karma and then to greater karma exercises.
Furthering through meditation, and deepening of the study	Furthering through study of karma and reincarnation teachings: eventually, karmic research
Philosophy of Freedom and *Knowledge of Higher Worlds*: the ideal individual development	*Mystery Dramas*: the individual development attained in concert with other human beings
Individual path	Social path
Adult Learning (Learning from the world) of Coen van Houten	Destiny Learning (Learning from Life) of Coen van Houten
3rd panel of the Foundation Stone Meditation	1st panel of the Foundation Stone Meditation
Understanding of the Spirit	Conscious experience of Destiny

Table 5: Spirit Beholding and Spirit Recollection

physical, mental, and spiritual health; looking at our shortcomings rather than those of others; realizing that thoughts and feelings are as important as deeds we do in the outer world; acquiring conviction of our soul-spiritual nature as the foundation of our true being; steadfastness to our outer and inner commitments and detachment from results; and developing a sense of gratitude for all that we receive. The seventh is a recapitulation and synthesis of the six. Likewise, in the same book, under the heading of "Inner Peace," what is presented has the same stamp as what was later presented in fuller detail with the karma exercises. "We should allow our joys, sorrows, worries, experiences, and actions to pass before our soul. But our attitude toward these should be one of looking at everything we have experienced from a higher point of view." Or further, "In the time we have set aside for ourselves, then, we must strive to view and judge our own experiences and actions as though they belonged to another person." And, "As students of higher knowledge, we must find the strength to view ourselves as we would view strangers." The above intentions that Steiner articulated at the early stage of the formulation of anthroposophy were amplified later in the karma exercises.

Techniques such as Nonviolent Communication or van den Brink's "helping conversation" offer tools for a true Goethean conversation, through an enhanced understanding of the archetypal social phenomenon. They offer individuals the possibility to take full responsibility for the circumstances of their incarnation, allowing them to reach the maturity of soul implied in the Lesser Karma Exercise. Coenraad van Houten's Destiny Learning can be equated to a Greater Karma Exercise that is carried with the help of a group and the guidance of a facilitator over four to five days. The practice allows us to reach the second part of the path of Spirit Recollection: retrieving knowledge of aspects of our previous lives, which follows the steps of taking responsibility for our own lives.

The path of Spirit Recollection promotes more particularly Inspiration. Let us look at present to what we could call an "Inspiration exercise" that Steiner outlined in *The Stages of Higher Knowledge*.[101]

---

[101] Steiner, *The Stages of Higher Knowledge*, Chapter: Inspiration.

Here we are asked to imagine a situation we are facing that carries an emotional charge. And we are told that if we can place ourselves in front of the situation in our mind's eye and imagine it as vividly as possible, we will be able to confront it differently. "This can be accomplished either by actually confronting such an experience, or by conjuring it up imaginatively. The imaginative method is even better for a really fruitful occult training." When we accomplish the exercise we deny ourselves the feelings that would normally be conjured up. If we have explored our responses in the inner encounter, when the real situation confronts us we will be able to face it with equanimity. All the energies that would otherwise have been dissipated in worry, anxiety, and fear are made available in the moment we previously would have dreaded, and an inspiration will be made available to us. Notice that this is not the attainment of Inspiration itself, but a stage on the way to it. This exercise is a step that is practiced regularly in various popular practical applications of Spirit Recollection, all the way from the Twelve Step program to Nonviolent Communication and Theory U that we will see in the next chapter. Spirit Recollection starts with review and recollection, and naturally ends in a preview in which one envisions events to come and how to confront them.

In the approaches and techniques of Spirit Recollection given by Prokofieff, van Houten, Salman, and others mentioned earlier, the disciplines and social tools are aimed at rendering the encounter more conscious. Social collaboration lies at the center of these approaches, as authors like Salman and van den Brink indicate about the social path.

Steiner's exercises form the larger archetype of what we have seen in the applications (tools for moral imagination) that have appeared particularly in van Houten and van den Brink's work. In van den Brink's "helping conversation," we can recognize the exercises Steiner gave that lead to the Lesser Karma Exercise. Everything we do individually in the Lesser Karma Exercises is done in the facilitated dialogue or enhanced conversation with another person. We start from recreating and reliving past events. We then elevate the experience, above all elements of sympathy or antipathy; and finally, we distill an extract, and promote the reverence and attitude of mind that fosters spiritual insight. In the end, we could say that what emerges from this conversation is very much the same as what we would retrieve from Steiner's exercises, up to the Lesser Karma Exercise. The insight that we formulate in a "potentized dialogue" is equivalent to what comes to the surface of consciousness after we practice Steiner's exercises repeatedly. Coenraad van Houten's Destiny Learning provides the complementary approach, which offers us access to the Greater Karma Exercise in conjunction with the use of the archetypal social phenomenon. Because the work considers a life event over four to five days, insights have a chance to mature over the course of the nights, and even provide us with the objective certainty of a previous life event, just as one can have when doing the Greater Karma Exercise.

From the above, we can outline two variations on the path of Spirit Recollection. The first lies in individual work through Steiner's exercises of Spirit Recollection, those we have mentioned earlier; the second uses the blueprint of these exercises, or their archetypes, in social activities involving two or more individuals. In Margret van den Brink and Coenraad van Houten's work, as well as in those techniques that lie outside of anthroposophy, the conscious and elaborate art of enhancing what naturally occurs in the archetypal social phenomenon serves as a support for connecting with the forces of destiny, and eventually opens the door for an understanding of root causes in previous lifetimes.

Our exploration of the impulse of Spirit Recollection would not be complete without touching even briefly on what lies in between Spirit Recollection and Spirit Beholding: Spirit Mindfulness or Spirit Awareness. We can only fully apprehend the first three panels of the Foundation Stone in relation to each other, and in relation to the fourth panel.

CHAPTER 6

SPIRIT MINDFULNESS, THE PATH TO THE CHRIST

The preceding section has examined the contrast between the first and third panels (or verses) of the Foundation Stone Meditation in relation to Spirit Recollection and Spirit Beholding. We can now attempt to complete the picture by turning our attention to the path of Spirit Mindfulness (or Spirit Sensing) in the second panel of the meditation.

In his *Anthroposophical Leading Thoughts* 66 to 68 Steiner outlined the three paths of the Foundation Stone without naming them; and he placed them in a different order. We will turn to this characterization, which offers us an entry point into the territory we want to explore.

Leading Thought 66 makes a statement that refers to the third panel: "The Beings of the Third Hierarchy reveal themselves in the life that is unfolded as a spiritual background in human Thinking. In the human activity of thought, this life is concealed. If it worked on in its own essence in human thought, humanity could not attain freedom. Where cosmic Thought-activity ceases, human Thought-activity begins." In this leading thought lies encapsulated the most well-known and best-understood of these processes: Spirit Beholding. This is the transformation of thinking, the human activity of beholding the thoughts of the spiritual world, which is rendered possible when all of our thinking has been transformed through the living assimilation of the teachings of anthroposophy.

99

To follow our line of thought, we will next examine the first panel, the characterization of Spirit Recollection. Leading Thought 68 states: "The Beings of the First Hierarchy manifest themselves in spiritual creation beyond humanity—a cosmic world of spiritual Being that indwells human Willing. This world of cosmic Spirit experiences itself in creative action when man wills. It first creates the connection of man's being with the Universe beyond humanity; only then does man himself become, through his organism of Will, a freely willing human being." It is precisely through the activity of Spirit Recollection that we are reminded of the words of Steiner in *Awakening to Community*: "... one succeeds in keeping the soul still while the body moves through space; succeeds in being active in the world while the soul remains quiet; carries activity and at the same time quietly observes it; then thinking suffuses the will, just as the will previously suffused thinking [referring to the Saturn Path or Spirit Beholding]."[102] Here is encapsulated the essence of Spirit Recollection, the path of the will through thinking.

Finally, the words of Leading Thought 67 express the level of experience that is accessible through the second panel: "The Beings of the Second Hierarchy manifest themselves in a world-of-soul beyond humanity—a world of cosmic soul-activities, hidden from human Feeling. This cosmic world-of-soul is ever creative in the background of human Feeling. Out of the being of man, it first creates the organism of Feeling; only then can it bring Feeling itself to life therein." In the correspondence to the panel of the Foundation Stone, this is where we find the expression of Spirit Mindfulness or Spirit Awareness.

Path to the Christ and the Cultivation of Feeling

When we refer to Spirit Mindfulness, we are moving into the space of the heart and lungs, in the experience and expression of purified feelings. In the lecture cycle *From Jesus to Christ*, Steiner offered a building element to this idea of purified feeling of the heart as a path to the Christ. In addition to the paths to the Christ through the Gospels on one side, and the path of esoteric revelation on the other, for modern times there

---

[102] Steiner, *Awakening to Community*, February 6, 1923 lecture.

is a path we will refer to as a "third path." Blaise Pascal and Vladimir Soloviev are both representatives of this third path. Steiner said that these two are part of a long line of men who have the new required feelings. This third way Steiner called the "Way of Self-Knowledge," and he added "as the witnesses cited [Pascal and Soloviev], together with thousands and thousands of other human beings can testify from their own experience, it leads to a recognition that self-knowledge in post-Christian time is impossible without placing Christ Jesus by the side of man...."[103]

Steiner linked this third path to conditions that are emerging at present. "Out of the large number of those who could be named I will mention only two [Pascal and Soloviev] who have given eminent testimony to the fact that Christ (Who from the twentieth century onward will be seen through the more highly developed faculties) can be *recognized, felt, experienced, through feelings* that were not possible in the same form before the Event of Golgotha."[104] Theirs are paths of "inner deepening of heart and soul" in which the "way must begin in experiences through feeling."[105]

In his *Pensées,* the French philosopher Pascal summed up that in feeling, we experience in relation to the divine either the extreme of pride and arrogance (the illusion that we are God), or of despair (not connecting to the divine at all). It is only in between these extremes that the soul can find what we could call the purified Christ-feeling. It is only in apprehending the reality of the Christ deed and the Christ being that we can live between the extremes. This is what leads to the birth of the new Christ event in our souls, at the time in which the Christ appears in the etheric.

The Russian mystic Soloviev pointed to two powers in the human soul between which the Christ mediates: one is immortality, the other wisdom or moral perfection. In nature (of which human nature shares the essence to start with), neither of these is found. All nature leads to

---

[103] Steiner, *From Jesus to Christ*, October 8, 1911 lecture.
[104] Steiner, *Esoteric Lessons, 1904-1909: Lectures, Notes, Meditations, and Exercises by Rudolf Steiner. Notes of Esoteric Lessons from Memory by the Participants*, 186 Record B of Esoteric Lesson of June 1, 1907 in Munich.
[105] Steiner, *Rosicrucian Wisdom*, June 6, 1907 lecture.

death; that is the only certainty of science. We carry the longing for immortality because we also have a striving for human perfection. But the latter would be rendered moot without the possibility for immortality. Going beyond death means reaching beyond the realm of nature, into what Soloviev called the "realm of Grace." Christ is the only one who can unite the realm of nature and the realm of Grace, and the only one who can offer us an answer. And the consciousness that leads us to the Christ is what Soloviev called faith. Soloviev saw faith as an act of necessity and an inner duty; he also saw it as an accomplishment that we cannot attain without a free act. Without believing in Christ we paralyze ourselves. If the historic Christ had not entered into evolution and given us the possibility of experiencing Him through faith, the soul would have to say to itself "I Am Not," rather than "I Am." The soul can recognize its true existence only by turning back through faith to the historic Jesus Christ. Here again, the Christ is the doorway to the reconciliation of polarities.

Christian Esoteric and Rosicrucian Paths

The modern path to Christ, on which Pascal and Soloviev are the forerunners, is a continuation of the seven stages of the Christian Initiation, as a path through the feelings, which has accompanied us into modern times alongside the more generally attainable Rosicrucian path. Contrary to an assumption that seems widespread in anthroposophic circles, this initiation is still valid today; but it is more difficult than the Rosicrucian.

Steiner is quite clear in numerous places about the co-existence of the two esoteric paths: the Christian and the Rosicrucian. "The Christian-esoteric training and the Christian-Rosicrucian training continue to exist in the West. The former trains through the feeling, the latter through the understanding."[106] A major difference between the two paths is their degree of accessibility. "The nature of Christian initiation involves passing through states of humility and devotion. Whoever pursues this with full seriousness, experiences his resurrection

---

[106] Steiner, *St. John Gospel*, May 31, 1908 lecture.

in the world of spirit. Today, not everyone is capable of doing this."[107] Continuing to let Steiner speak for the issue, we come to the point of the different requests that the two paths place on individuals: "It [Christian initiation] requires withdrawing from other people for certain periods. But the Rosicrucian method exists precisely to enable people to work their way upward into higher worlds without neglecting their everyday obligations."[108] And further:

> These [Christian and Rosicrucian] are the two paths of esoteric training particularly fitted for the West. All that is connected with our culture and the life we lead and must lead, is lifted up, raised into the principle of initiation through the Christian and through the Rosicrucian training. The purely Christian way is somewhat difficult for modern human beings; hence the Rosicrucian path has been introduced for those who have to live in the present age. If someone wants to take the old, purely Christian, path in the midst of modern life, he must be able to cut himself off for a time from the world outside, in order to enter it again later all the more intensely.[109]

And finally, the Christian path asks for a prerequisite understanding of Christianity that the Rosicrucian path does not require. On this Christian path, the Gospel of Saint John plays a central role as a path of meditation, and hence it can be trod only with a deep conviction of, and devotion to, the divinity of Christ.[110] All of these elements together explain the assumption that the Christian esoteric stream is not appropriate for our times.

---

[107] Steiner, *Rosicrucian Wisdom*, June 6, 1907 lecture.

[108] Ibid.

[109] Steiner, *The First Esoteric Class after the separation from the Esoteric School of theosophy, on the separation of the Eastern and Western Schools*, Munich, June 1, 1907, notes from Steiner, 289.

[110] Steiner, *Rosicrucian Wisdom*, June 6, 1907 lecture.

The misunderstanding that the Christian path was valid only during the Middle Ages (an assumption that this author carried himself) arises from a variety of factors. It is a more exacting, more difficult path, and is not appropriate for everyone. First of all let us see how, from Steiner's perspective, the two are related historically. "The Master Jesus [the reincarnated Zarathustra who received the Christ-baptism at the Jordan] and the Master Christian Rosenkreutz have prepared two paths of initiation for us: the Christian-Esoteric path and the Christian-Rosicrucian one. These two paths have existed ever since the Middle Ages."[111] This is a first layer of the present question. In contrasting the two paths, Steiner offers: "The Christian path is more an inward one, while in Rosicrucian schooling one's feelings are kindled through the external world."[112] In the Christian path of initiation, "the human being experiences in the astral realm what we find described in the Gospel of Saint John as 'historical fact.'"[113]

In the lecture cycle on the Gospel of Saint John, Steiner characterizes the Christian path as that of the feeling life, in contrast to the Rosicrucian as a "combination of feeling and will."[114] That this quote seems to contradict the previous one above (in which the Rosicrucian path is referred to the "understanding") is only an apparent contradiction. Thinking and will continuously interpenetrate each other. The Rosicrucian path makes an appeal to the understanding through the element of the will. At the same time, it appeals to the realm of feelings.

The Christian esoteric path comprises the following stages: Washing of the Feet, Scourging, Crowning with Thorns, Mystic Death, Burial, Resurrection, and Ascension. Through enhanced feeling an Imagination is created, leading to an experience that eventually reaches the physical body in order to be complete. In the Washing of the Feet, the experience is reached in which one would feel as if water were washing over the feet. In the next step the individual would experience "something like sharp pains and wounding, like strokes of a scourge against his own

---

[111] Steiner, *St. John Gospel*, May 31, 1908 lecture.
[112] Ibid, May 30, 1908 lecture.
[113] Steiner, *From Jesus to Christ*, October 14, 1911 lecture.
[114] Steiner, *The East in the Light of the West*, August 28, 1909 lecture.

skin, and the Imagination arises as if he were outside himself, scourged, according to the example of Christ Jesus."[115] Through a penetration of the feelings down into the physical body, the result of the path is the attainment of a state in which the individual can acquire a concrete experience of strength and freedom that enhances his capacity for acts of love and devotion.

Although the Rosicrucian path is markedly different from the Christian esoteric path, there is a certain similarity between the two in what concerns the understanding of the Christ Mystery. The part of the Rosicrucian path that leads to the Christ emphasizes a purification of feelings. The Rosicrucian initiate directed his attention to the Christ through immersion in the texts of the Gospels, particularly the Gospel of Saint John, which is also central to the Christian esoteric path. In this way the mystical, inner Christ was awakened. "Feelings more especially are purified in this way."[116] The initiate found his way to what the spiritual world offered to the soul through the fact that the Christ had descended from the macrocosm at Golgotha. "If their feelings are aglow with enthusiasm for the divine as soon as they are permeated with the Christ substance, the other faculties through which we understand the world are illuminated and strengthened by the Luciferic principle." This reference is to the positive Luciferic principle, which offers deeper understanding of Christ. Through the Luciferic principle one would not simply meet the Christ, but acquire the ability to understand and characterize the experience.

That the experience of the Christ is reached primarily, and more

---

[115] Steiner, *Mysteries of Light, of Space and of the Earth*, December 13, 1919 lecture.
[116] Steiner, *Karmic Relationships*, Volume 3, July 28 lecture. Here we are told, "Christ, the lofty Spirit of the Sun, is arriving on earth, incarnating in the human being Jesus of Nazareth. Those who dwell on the earth experience the fact that Christ, the great Spirit of the Sun, arrives among them. But they have little knowledge that could really cause them to understand the greatness of the stupendous and unique event.

All the more knowledge have those disembodied souls who are gathered around Michael and who are living in the realm of the Sun-existence in worlds above the earth."

fully, in the realm of feelings, is also confirmed in relation to what Steiner had to say in December of 1919 about the sculptural group of the Representative of Humanity before it was sculpted. This is what he says in relation to the Christ figure, which holds the balance between Ahriman and Lucifer, "But this has to be felt in an artistic way. It must not merely be thought of intellectually in some weird and wonderful way. But it has to be felt." And further: "Nevertheless it is essential that entirely out of the feelings—that is, excluding the intellect altogether, for that is meant to be only the means for reaching feeling—people shall be urged to look toward the east [where the Representative of Humanity stood] and be able to say 'That is you.'"[117] And the whole of the Group is supposed to work as an after-image in the realm of feelings, indicating to us how the Christ places Himself as a balance between Lucifer and Ahriman.

Let us finally place the path of Spirit Mindfulness in the context of the second panel of the Foundation Stone Meditation.

Soul of man!
Thou livest in the beat of Heart and Lung
Which leads thee through the rhythmic tides of time
Into the feeling of your own Soul-being:
Practice Spirit-mindfulness
In balance of the soul
Where the surging
Deeds of the World's becoming
Do thine own I
Unite
Unto the I of the World.
Then mid the weaving of the Soul of Man
Thou will truly feel.

For the Christ-Will in the encircling Rounds holds sway
In the Rhythms of Worlds, blessing the Soul.
Kyriotetes, Dynamis, Exusiai,

---

[117] Steiner, *Rosicrucianism and Modern Initiation*, January 13, 1924 lecture.

You Spirits of Light!
Let there be fired from the East
What through the West is formed,
Speaking:
In Christo Morimur.
The elemental Spirits hear
In East and West and North and South
May human beings hear it!

What has been previously explored is here confirmed. It is in Spirit Mindfulness (Sensing) that we meet the Christ, mentioned here twice, and implied once more in the expression "I of the world," while His name doesn't appear in the first and third panels of the meditation. And the experience of Christ is intimately connected with the human being's rhythmic system, with balance of the soul and with feeling ("truly feel"). It is in and through Christ that we can truly feel, as the examples of Pascal and Soloviev demonstrate.

Leading Thought 67 confirms this link between Second Hierarchy and Soul Activities thus: "The Beings of the Second Hierarchy manifest themselves in a world-of-soul beyond humanity—a world of cosmic-soul-activities, hidden from human Feeling. This cosmic world-of-soul is ever creative in the background of human Feeling. Out of the being of man it first creates the organism of Feeling; only then can it bring Feeling itself to life therein."

We have come to the end of our exploration of the three paths of the Foundation Stone Meditation. To conclude we want to return to the words of Zeylmans van Emmichoven—a lifelong researcher of the Christmas Meeting and of the Foundation Stone Meditation—and complete what we have quoted from him in Chapter 5: "'Practice spirit remembering [recollection]' not only means that we learn how our own 'I' is part of God's 'I'—no, out of cosmic heights we hear resound: 'From the divine, humanity takes its existence,' the humanity together with which we must come to a brotherly, social community. Thus 'Practice spirit reflection [mindfulness]' is a path of schooling for meeting the being of Christ, the cosmic ego, the 'I' of humanity, to which in the far-distant future all human beings can find their free relationship. The third task set us, 'Practice spirit vision [beholding],' is ultimately the path from natural science to spiritual science, from anthropology to anthroposophy."[118]

---

[118] Zeylmans von Emmichoven, *An Inspiration for Anthroposophy*, 249.

CHAPTER 7

EXPLORATION OF THE IMPULSE OF SPIRIT RECOLLECTION

In Chapter 4 we have explored the impulse of Spirit Recollection from the perspective of the karmic exercises, through which we bring to life the perception of the forces of destiny, the reality of karma and reincarnation. These were summarized on table 4.

We will now briefly recapitulate the findings of that chapter. The basic exercise of Spirit Recollection is expressed by the rückschau. It is the activity of living the course of time backwards, most typically reviewing the day. It strengthens our ability to enter the reality of the etheric body, our "time body." The next step consists in looking back at our life or at the expression of someone else's being. We can either look back at a time in our life, or try to bring to life what is essential to the soul make-up and deeper essence of another human being. The first activity requires from us to be both participants and spectators in our own lives, and ultimately see ourselves with detachment. When we look back at a time in our lives—be this the last weeks or months, or a period of years further back in time—we become able to lift our ego from too close an identification with the events of our biography. In other words, we develop a clear understanding that our individuality, the deeper essence of who we are, is but partly expressed by the events of our biography; and furthermore, that the setbacks we have encountered on our life course need not condition who we will be in the future.

Looking at another human being more fully means being able to recreate, through sense impressions and through memory, who this human being truly is, and what he or she has contributed to our lives. It is an effort that finds its completion in the forming of a true imagination. Over time such an effort modifies our perceptions in two ways, if not more. First of all, we will see our life as the tapestry of manifold contributions, and learn to be less self-referential. Secondly, we will increase interest in our fellow human being.

A further stage along the path of Spirit Recollection is represented by the lesser karma exercise. Through such an inner activity we no longer simply look back to events in our lives. We introduce some key concepts of karma and reincarnation. First among these is the notion that we are actively seeking ways in our lives to honor our pre-birth resolves, strengthen our individuality and meet obligations we have brought forth from previous lives. The exercise asks us to imagine that an undesired event in our life is such only in appearance; in reality the 'second man in us' (our higher self) has actively willed this event into our lives. We are asked to imagines ourselves, as vividly as possible, preparing the event in order to willingly undergo its consequences. When this is done over and over again, the human being naturally understands that what meets her in this life is what she has willed, not random chance. This is an almost complete reversal from ordinary consciousness. The individual can therefore start to take responsibility for her life rather than escape its lessons by projecting blame upon others.

Interiorizing the lesser karma exercise is a milestone in Spirit Recollection. No theoretical notions of karma and reincarnation will familiarize us with forces of destiny; we can start to experience these forces in our very own lives only through inner effort and reflection upon our life experiences. And this is the prerequisite for breaking through the veil of maya concerning our relationships on earth.

The idea that we are responsible for what comes to us in life naturally leads to the question "what is meeting me at key moments of my life, at particularly important turning points, and in recurring events that seem to form a pattern?" The greater karma exercise consists of looking at an event over three nights. Once again, we bring back to memory everything that has met us in the senses in relation to a particular event.

Many attempts may be necessary before we are eventually able to behold events from previous lifetimes, which are connected with what happens to us in the present. This exercise forms the pinnacle of the activity of Spirit Recollection.

Spirit Recollection is the activity of moving back in time, as the term recollection itself indicates. As the realm of space is ruled by the number twelve, so is the activity in time based on the number seven. Examples of the latter are the days of the week, the length of the phases of life (birth to seven years, seven to fourteen, fourteen to twenty-one, etc.), the cycles of evolution (the seven Atlantean ages, the seven post-Atlantean ages, etc.).

Seven is the number of the life processes. We have encountered these in the moral technique known as Destiny Learning, which was described in Chapter 3. This was a first revelation in my biographical journey. The second came through Otto Scharmer's Theory U in something seemingly very different from Destiny Learning; here, we find again seven stages at work in the U-shaped curve that is central to Theory U. Scharmer's work no longer addresses individual biographical processes, as does Destiny Learning, but organizational/social processes. The similarities are therefore not immediately apparent. They lie in the fact that organizations of any size have a development in time, and therefore a biography. Theory U is an organizational biographic process that leads to the emergence of a higher common consciousness and to decision-making of a unique kind. Theory U, as we will see at the end of this exploration, also passes through the central stage of individualization, which receives the name of 'presencing.'

After studying the role of the seven life processes in the two instances above, I started to recognize that the sevenfold pattern is everywhere at work in individual and collective experiential processes leading to personal or organizational growth. The seven life processes seem to emerge organically, and they can be recognized when one immerses oneself deeply in many of the existing moral techniques. In this chapter we will refer to some of the best well-known, or of the most emblematic. But many others could have been given instead.

One immediate difference arises between individual processes and those referring to groups and organizations. At the individual level we can pierce through the veil of maya completely; we can reach the recognition of previous life events, as is the case in the greater karma exercise. In the case of group and organizational work we can only go as far as the lesser karma exercise, the stage of taking responsibility for our lives.

The work of Spirit Recollection can also be referred to with the name "experiential spirituality." Such experiential work does not necessitate knowledge of anthroposophy as a prerequisite, though this knowledge is used in some instances, particularly in such approaches as biography work and Destiny Learning. On the other hand, karmic research—to which we will return at the end of the chapter—would not be possible without an anthroposophical understanding of the world. In the following pages I will only report approaches that I have experienced and investigated to a large degree. We will begin with a reminder about the seven life processes.

The Seven Life Processes and Spirit Recollection

The seven life processes are breathing, warming, nourishing, secreting, maintaining, growing, and reproducing. There is a process of breathing, of warming, of nourishing, and so forth, for our seeing, hearing, sense of balance, and each of the twelve senses.

The first three processes (breathing, warming, and nourishing) reach us in the interaction with the external world. The process of secreting concerns the internal secretion that facilitates assimilation and absorption and also excretion. The last three processes characterize the inner life of every organism. What is taken from the world by the organism first sustains maintenance, then growth, and finally reproduction. The seven life processes build the sheaths of the human being, and are progressively released for soul-spiritual processes. It is to those that we turn below.

In this chapter will be presented various approaches that use the seven life processes. Some of these have done so deliberately (Destiny Learning and biography work). The others (the Twelve Step program and Nonviolent Communication) have evolved organically, incorporating *de facto* what can be expressed through the seven life processes. They are the result of processes elaborated through group work and wisdom over extended periods of time.

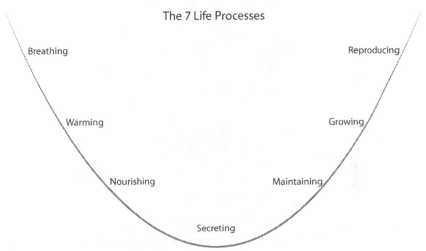

Table 6: The Seven Life Processes

The Breadth of the Impulse of Spirit Recollection

What will be presented below has come to the surface from the author's explorations and personal exposure. Table 7 is only a convenient way to offer an overview of the extent of human experience that experiential spirituality covers.

The techniques have been ordered in such a way as to progress in depth (quality of the insights generated culminating in knowledge of previous lifetimes' experiences) on the horizontal axis, and in width (number of people that can be affected) on the vertical axis. On the horizontal axis we move from subjective to objective knowledge in a way that will be made apparent shortly. On the vertical axis we move from work geared for the sake of the individual, to work meant for larger and larger wholes: communities, organizations, networks. We should keep in mind that this is only a device for making trends more visible, and that there is no way to quantify the position of any given technique along these coordinates. It is to be expected that different people will make significantly different judgments in this regard.

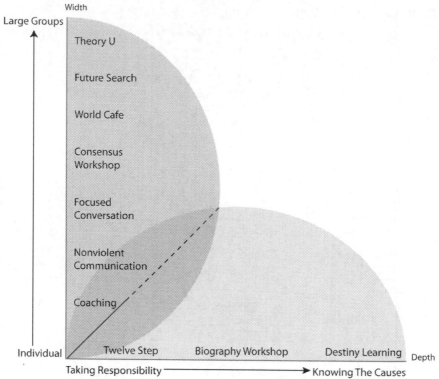

Table 7: The Field of Experiential Spirituality

Individual Work

Let us start with work done with individuals. Two such examples can be mentioned: life-coaching, and the work of the various Twelve Step programs (Alcoholics Anonymous [AA] was the first and most well-known of these).

Coaching is a lighter version of counseling, less therapeutic and more goal-oriented. The individual who turns to a coach wants to align her life with her personal values; to have a source of support and someone who will hold her accountable to her commitments. Much of the coaching is determined by inquiries, assignments to be carried outside of the coaching session, and changes of attitude and beliefs.

Twelve Step refers to the specific stages that first emerged in the formulation of the Alcoholics Anonymous process. Its official twelve steps are:

Step 1:   We admitted we were powerless over alcohol—that our lives had become unmanageable.

Step 2:   Came to believe that a Power greater than ourselves could restore us to sanity.

Step 3:   Made a decision to turn our will and our lives to the care of God as we understood him.

Step 4:   Made a searching and fearless moral inventory of ourselves.

Step 5:   Admitted to God, ourselves, and to another human being the exact nature of our wrongs.

Step 6:   Were entirely ready to have God remove all these defects of character.

Step 7:   Humbly asked him to remove our shortcomings.

Step 8:   Made a list of all persons we harmed, and became willing to make amends to them all.

Step 9:   Made direct amends to such people wherever possible, except when to do so would injure them or others.

Step 10: Continued to take personal inventory, and when we were wrong promptly admitted it.

Step 11: Sought through prayer and meditation to improve our conscious contact with God as we understood Him, praying only for knowledge of His will for us and the power to carry it out.

Step 12: Having had a spiritual awakening as the result of these steps, we tried to carry the message to alcoholics, and to practice these principles in all our affairs.[119]

---

[119] For further information on Twelve Step, its history and development, see Alcoholics Anonymous World Services, *Alcoholics Anonymous: The Story of How Many Thousands of Men and Women Have Recovered from Alcoholism,* and Alcoholics Anonymous World Services, *Twelve Steps and Twelve Traditions.*

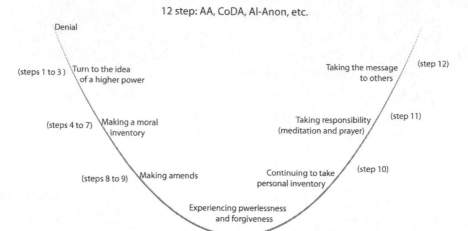

Table 8: Twelve Step in Relation to the Seven Life Processes

The whole life of an alcoholic or addict is an endless, repetitive act of denial of reality. Initiating the Twelve Step process means being willing to acknowledge our powerlessness and open up to the idea of a higher power (steps one to three). This is just the first breach in the armor that surrounds the addict and that nullifies all his well-meaning efforts. It concerns the intellect. A second significant step comes from the individual's involving herself with an open heart in making a moral inventory and letting herself be touched in her feelings through an understanding of the pain she has caused to others (steps three to seven), thereby acquiring new faculties of empathy. Finally, at steps eight and nine the candidate jumps into the crucible of the transformation of her will when she goes through the zero point of making herself completely vulnerable and powerless, in making amends to all those she has hurt. This is truly a turning point, a seeming place of void that opens new doors. Past and future meet in the willingness to make oneself truly powerless; but new, deeper power emerges that connects an individual with her higher self and with what the future is calling her to become.

In all the successive stages the individual goes from being supported by the organization to becoming an active supporter and shaper. At step ten what has been taken from the previous stages becomes an ongoing practice. This is what allows the point of openness to the future to become a source of continuous inspiration. The text mentions "continued to take personal inventory and when we were wrong promptly admitted it." The individual does not experience the stage of openness to the future only once, and then leave it, but must return to it over and over again. Step eleven means fully taking responsibility for our lives and being able to carry others, part of which is the taking up of an active discipline of prayer and meditation. The recovering addict is now putting his "shoulder to the wheel"; not only for his personal recovery, but also for the good of the group, and eventually of the Twelve Step program itself. Finally, there is in step twelve the complete dedication to and adoption in daily life of the goals of the Twelve Step process ("carrying the message to alcoholics and practicing the twelve steps in all affairs"), which means contributing to the continuance and regeneration of the group. Not surprisingly, from the accrued effects of all these steps practiced by thousands of individuals over many decades, AA is effective not only in its group work, but it is also very innovative, solid, and efficient in its organizational structure. The Twelve Step program can be seen as a way to change a given "double" (a particular manifestation of the larger double), and as an expression of Steiner's Lesser Karma Exercise.

Destiny Learning (mentioned in Chapter 3) attains the furthest reaches of individual work. It allows individuals to reach glimpses of previous life experiences, albeit very limited in scope, thus deepening understanding of karma and reincarnation, and reawakening individual pre-birth resolves.

Group Work

Let us move one step further, with Nonviolent Communication (NVC), which is undoubtedly a tool for self-improvement. It is also the quintessential tool of the encounter occurring between two individuals or two groups. In NVC, we pay attention to the expression of communication as it differentiates itself in observations, feelings, needs, and requests, by learning to express those in terms that derive from the expression of our higher self; and we learn to recognize when their expression is tainted by the content of our double(s). We learn therefore to take responsibility for the way we use language; the main corrective is to express ourselves more coherently (outwardly and inwardly), rather than falling into finding blame in another person.

Nonviolent Communication endeavors to render communication objective. It recognizes four levels to a conversation: description of facts or observation, expression of feelings, expression of needs, and formulation of requests.[120] We will consider the case of a mediation, because it illustrates most clearly the process of Nonviolent Communication. An NVC mediation is a process in which participants are helped in forming a true connection at the level of feelings and will before having to take on any decision. It is not a place of compromise, but a true shift to a higher level, marked by the active presence of the higher selves. A true NVC mediation can only occur after the participants experience a qualitative shift in themselves and in the relationship.

At the beginning of the process the participants are "behaving in jackal," an NVC term that means repeating past perceptions and behaviors. The situation is stuck; there is only a conversation between doubles. ("Double" is the closest anthroposophic term for the playful NVC "jackal.")

The mediator receives the participants, who are called "conflictants," and explains to them how the group process will lead them to interact with each other through his help. Basically this means he helps them each "reflect" what the other has said. In order to ensure reaching this goal, the mediator often verbally reflects what the other party says, feels, and wants, waiting for each party to repeat what the mediator said, in their own words.

At a first level, the mediator helps the participants refrain from bringing in past events. Those are known beforehand. Only those events that concern the mediation moment are looked at. This is a stage of grounding in objective truth. The past is already layered with interpretation, and cannot be counted on to add objective common ground. The two parties are invited to express each other's feelings and needs, and the mediator ensures that each is heard by the other. Basically, party A expresses himself, the mediator extracts the feelings and needs, and restates A's position. He then asks party B to repeat

---

[120] Marshall B. Rosenberg, *Nonviolent Communication: A Language of Compassion.*

what he has heard in terms of A's feelings and needs. The same process is repeated for party B, and the process continues for as long as there is a felt need from the participants.

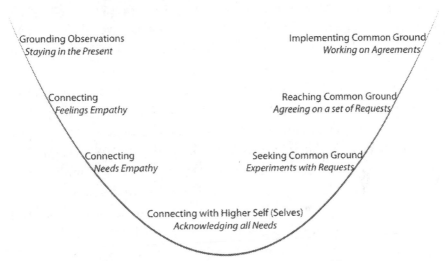

Grounding Observations
Staying in the Present

Implementing Common Ground
Working on Agreements

Connecting
Feelings Empathy

Reaching Common Ground
Agreeing on a set of Requests

Connecting
Needs Empathy

Seeking Common Ground
Experiments with Requests

Connecting with Higher Self (Selves)
Acknowledging all Needs

Table 9: NVC Mediation in Relation to the Seven Life Processes

If all goes well, the participants reach a point of breakthrough, which can be noticed because there is a slowing in the pace of mediation, the participants acting noticeably more relaxed, breathing deeply, waiting for the next step. Most likely this stage will be reached only through iterations, requiring a return to the previous stages, particularly as new feelings, corresponding to new needs, emerge. Once the shift has been reached in a permanent way, then the mediator can work at finding common ground. Requests are put out in a sort of brainstorming session in which anything is possible. From these only the most concrete and doable emerge, through which the participants agree that they can meet all their respective needs. Finally the results obtained must be implemented and stand the test of time. At this stage there can be a solution; further negotiations between the parties on new agreements; or return, at a higher level, to mediation.

We could say that mediation is a way to transform the "doubles" of the participants and of the relationship by bringing out the higher selves in both participants.

Organizational Work

At a higher stage, one can involve a whole community or organization. This has been done with techniques too many to name here that can be grouped under the general label "social technology": Appreciative Inquiry, Technology of Participation, Future Search, World Cafe, Open Space Technology, and so forth. To involve a group in decisions that generate the collaboration of all parties, these techniques build on a series of polarities and rhythms: rhythm of day and night; emphasis on past, present and future; movement from complexity to simplicity; from large to small groups; from single stakeholder groups to mixed groups; from individual to group work; analytical and imaginative activities, and so forth. To be effective, these techniques emphasize as diverse a participation as possible; a spirit of inclusion and participation; suspension of judgment; willingness to look at the whole picture, both good and bad; openness to the new, and so forth. The solutions will work when all individuals reach a stage in which they agree that they are all part of the problem, and that together they can contribute to the solution. This is the step of collectively taking responsibility for the situation at hand.

Many of the above techniques can be used at larger and larger levels, often in combination, to bring together networks of organizations around a concerted effort. Initiatives promoting sustainability across public, private, and non-profit sectors are an example of this. Worth mentioning at this level is Theory U, which is not a finite format, but an overall set of ideas that can be flexibly applied to create ad hoc formats fitting variable needs. Similar results can be obtained by variously combining the use of the various techniques mentioned above.

What NVC achieves for two individuals and eventually for the groups they represent (that is, mediation for two parties in conflict can take place between two of their representatives), social technology does for organizations or communities. Examples of social technology are Appreciative Inquiry, World Café, Future Search, Dynamic Facilitation, Technology of Participation, and so forth. In Otto Scharmer's *Theory U* an archetypal model is made manifest. All the social technologies listed earlier operate from this model. We will now look at one of the simplest interventions to help us hold a conversation (Focused Conversation), and at an approach that can be used at the highest levels of organizational complexity (Theory U).

Focused Conversation

This format creates the conditions in which a group of people may turn to a way of separating the essential from the non-essential, in discussing a general topic or exploring an agenda item in a meeting.[121] Participants learn to explore how any given situation has objective external factors; how the situation may cause internal reactions that cloud an objective relation to and understanding of it; how the situation needs to be thoroughly understood; and how decision-making depends on all the previous elements. More specifically these are the stages of the conversation:

Objective Level: a key word is "what." These are sensory questions. It is important not to downplay them. One has to face initial resistance and go through it with courage and persistence. This corresponds to the breathing life process. Key questions are: "What objects do you see?"; "What happened?"; "What words and sentences stand out?"

Reflective Level: a key word is "how." It serves to integrate right brain with left brain, and corresponds to the warming life process. Key questions are: "What does it remind you of?"; "How does it make you feel?"; "Where were you surprised?"; "…or delighted?"; "Where did you struggle?"

Interpretive Level: a key word is "why?" This is the level that may take the most time. It corresponds to the life process of nourishing. Key questions are: "What is happening?"; "What is this all about?"; "How will this affect us?" "What are we learning from this?"

---

[121] Brian Stanfield, *The Art of Focused Conversation: 100 Ways to Access Group Wisdom in the Workplace.*

The stage of individuation is seldom mentioned; when so, it is called the "Maieutic level" (from the Greek "giving birth").[122] In a study group this is the time of generating insight. In a decision-oriented conversation this is the moment when the group reaches consensus.

<u>Decisional level</u>: key words are "what, who, when, where." It corresponds to the two levels of maintaining and growing. And key questions are: "What is our response?"; "What decision is called for?"; "What are the next steps?"; "What changes will be required of us?"

The last stage is not considered in the Focused Conversation.

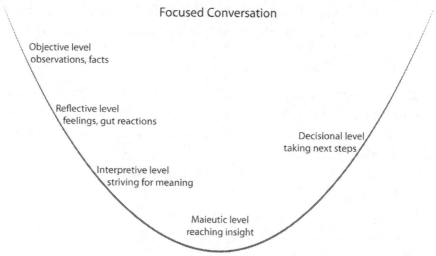

Table 10: Focused Conversation

By going through these steps in sequence, in many possible variations according to the matter at hand, the group is led to a place in which the conversation can be owned by all, and can naturally lead to results to which all can subscribe. The group will eventually take responsibility for their joint analysis/review of an event or action, for a study topic, or for joint decision-making.

---

[122] Jean Watts, *Guided Dialogue For Releasing Depth Wisdom*, at http://wikifoundryattachments.com/-3lwFFV7xW6uYeMw-Y9RMw72928

Theory U

Theory U posits that organizational and social change follows an archetypal seven-step process.[123] The first step in working with an organization or community is helping it to see things differently. When we are part of an organization, we daily inhale its patterns, and become blind to how they shape us. Usually we find outlets in blaming the CEO, other people in positions of authority, our colleagues, and/or external forces.

When all the significant stakeholders in a situation are called to express their views in settings and contexts that encourage true dialogue, people can finally see the tapestry of elements that contribute to form a situation of conflict. Clarity is reached about the complexity of factors that contribute to a given group dynamic. This is the stage of the Open Mind (See Table 11). From this first level, the participants can start to see patterns emerging and realize that they have unconsciously been part of them. Individuals and groups are encouraged to take responsibility for their part in the collective patterns. This is what encourages connection between stakeholders at the level of feelings, and what Otto Scharmer, originator of Theory U, calls the work of the Open Heart. When the process is completed, the shift is perceived in that the participants acknowledge a common ground from which they can operate, allied with a new enthusiasm and desire for moving into concerted action. This stage, in which the new can finally emerge, is called "presencing." For that to happen, all individuals must reach the willingness to let go of everything that they wanted beforehand, and trust the process and the wisdom that is present in the whole. Presencing is made possible through the Open Will. It is a place where the past is as if put on hold, and the participants can collectively listen to the future wanting to emerge. Letting go makes room for a process of allowing, or in Scharmer's words, "letting come."

---

[123] Otto Scharmer, *Theory U: Leading from the Emerging Future; The Social Technology of Presencing.*

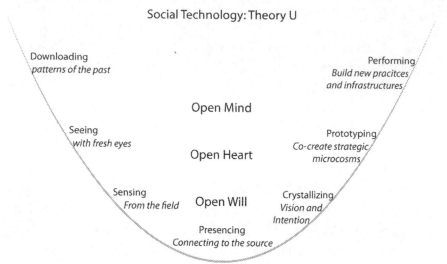

Table 11: Steps in Theory U

After presencing, the group moves into the right side of the U. At the stage of crystallizing, what emerges as an insight, a simple place of openness, almost a place of vacuum in the idea of presencing, needs to acquire focus and direction. Ideas need to be built upon and solidified, key players need to find each other and determine what forms their initiatives should take.

At the next stage, Theory U introduces the idea of prototyping, which means nurturing and sustaining pilot initiatives for testing concrete ideas on a small scale, and offering these all the needed support in order to later integrate the practices on larger scales. When pilot initiatives are successful, change is then brought to the level of the entire organization (performing). But performing means more than integrating the new. It means ensuring that the processes described before are sustained on an ongoing basis, particularly seeing, sensing, and presencing. For that purpose, the organization must set in place structures and processes that allow teams and organization again to go through collective experiences of seeing, sensing, and presencing, when needed.

Theory U and other similar applications do not address individual doubles. That process would be time-consuming and sterile on a large and complex scale of operation. Rather, in a sense, we could say that these group processes call upon the being of the organization in order to enable it to see its larger double, and modify it by degrees.

Theory U could be described as a tool that allows organizations to work beyond the blockages of some of its "collective doubles," by working through to what Steiner called the "new group soul."

Commonalities on the Path of Spirit Recollection

What unites all of these approaches to individual and social change? We can examine them as a whole first, and then discover the essence of these approaches. Most of them were developed rather instinctively, and are not based on an extensive body of knowledge; most often they were developed collectively. Those who engage in their use, especially as recipients, are asked simply to be willing to work with certain basic sets of experiences. It is through engaging the will that the individual or the group can start evolving new ways of thinking, and of seeing self, group or corporate identity under a new light. Much of this work requires a willingness to act differently than out of old habits, then to review and learn from the new actions and to deepen new habits in the will.

All of these approaches somehow call us to cultivate a historical consciousness. In the Twelve Step programs, the addicted individual retraces his biography in relation to the phenomenon of addiction; most so-called social technology requires the willingness to look at corporate history and to discern failures and successes. However, these are not "deficit" approaches; invariably the focus is placed on resources, strengths, and ability to awaken to one's own responsibilities, as being the engine that drives change.

We could say that all the approaches mentioned allow individuals or groups to develop, strengthen, or enable moral imagination through moral technique. In *Philosophy of Freedom*, Chapter 12, Steiner makes a distinction between "moral imagination" and "moral technique." He explains that having a strong moral imagination does not mean necessarily being able to communicate these imaginations to our fellow human being. There is a step between what we envision and what we convey to others, which requires a process of translation. An individual may have a strong capacity to live in a world of ideas, and to see their implications in the social realm, but may not know how to speak to another human being in a way that fully respects her freedom; or may not know how to convey his views with clarity, how to inspire the recipient with interest or enthusiasm, and so forth. The contrary is also true: someone may lack the capacity to live in ideas or form larger moral imaginations. However, he may be able to understand ideas that others articulate, and may be able to convey them effectively to others. This second person has the moral technique that is lacking in the first one. We could say that the whole of experiential spirituality and social technology is the field in which we learn to align moral imagination with moral technique.

One example will suffice. Through Nonviolent Communication, one easily sees that communication can be blocked at any of four levels of observations, feelings, needs or requests. At the first level, I may state an observation mixed with interpretation; at the second, express a feeling mixed with judgment; at the third level, express a need mixed with the strategies aiming at fulfilling it; at the fourth level, articulate an open request that sounds very similar to a demand. Mastering all of Nonviolent Communication inwardly means developing a capacity for being both honest with oneself and empathic with other people. But the ultimate litmus test arrives at the moment in which we articulate effectively each of the four elements of the conversation, and test the reaction in the other person. Increasing our capacity for honesty and empathy corresponds to the element of moral imagination. Conveying both effectively requires moral technique. Awareness alone is not sufficient.

None of the approaches listed in this chapter are "spiritual" per se, nor do they require subscribing to any set of beliefs, not even in the instance of Destiny Learning. Yet, it is very often the case that individuals engaged in repeated use of these approaches realize their spiritual dimension, sometimes in dramatic ways, as a result of key experiences. The spiritual dimension is shown in the expressions that have been adopted over time. In Appreciative Inquiry, the end of the process culminates in the "Destiny Phase"; this name was adapted over time in preference to the more prosaic "Delivery Phase," to denote the reality of the change set in motion through which the whole organization finds more of its essential being. And World Cafe speaks of "the magic in the middle," or of "the voice in the middle of the room" to refer to the presence that emerges as being larger than the sum of the parts. In Theory U, the turning point of group work is the moment in which individuals can experience the two streams of time: one stream coming from the past, and one coming from the future in what has been called "presencing." At this juncture, everyone can sense more of who they truly are, while at the same time experiencing harmony with what is willed by the group, or rather by the "spirit of the group." In anthroposophic terms, we are dealing with what Steiner called the "new group souls," who are active where people work together harmoniously.

Presencing is an all-encompassing experience; any single individual can apprehend only a facet. It is such a rich experience that everyone has a deeply personal way of expressing it. "When I am part of a social field that crosses the threshold at the bottom of the U, it feels as if I am participating in the birth of a new world. It is a profound, quieting experience; I feel as if I've been touched by eternal beauty. There is a deep opening of my higher Self," offers Betty Sue Flowers. For Joseph Jaworski, "...moving through the bottom of the U is becoming aware of the incredible beauty of life itself, of becoming re-enchanted with the world. ... When the sort of commitment you are talking about happens, you feel as if you're fulfilling your destiny, but you also feel as if you're freer than you've ever been in your life. It's a huge paradox." Otto Scharmer says: "For me, the core of presencing is waking up together—waking up to who we really are by linking with and acting from our highest future Self—and by using the Self as a vehicle for bringing forth new worlds."[124]

Steiner expressed the idea that we can let the "new group soul" speak through a gathering of people who can create a vessel of trust among themselves, and render it effective for work in the world. "Later [in the future] we shall live in the connections and associations that men create for themselves, uniting in groups with those of similar

---

[124] Peter Senge, C. Otto Scharmer, Joseph Jaworski, Betty Sue Flowers, *Presence: Exploring Profound Change in People, Organizations and Society*, 111, 113, 222 and 234.

ideas while retaining their complete freedom and individuality. To realize this is necessary for a right understanding of something like the Anthroposophical Society. The Anthroposophical Society is intended to be a first example of such a voluntary association, although we may be well aware that it has not yet reached very far."[125] And further in the same lecture cycle:

> But when men find themselves together in voluntary associations, they group themselves around centers. The feelings streaming in this way to a center once more give [spiritual] beings the opportunity of working as a kind of group soul, though in a quite different way from the early group souls. ... These new beings, however, are compatible with man's complete freedom and individuality. Indeed, in a certain respect we may say that they support their existence on human harmony; it will lie in the souls of men themselves whether or not they give as many as possible of such higher souls the opportunity of descending to man ... The more that associations are formed where feelings of fellowship are developed with complete freedom, the more lofty beings will descend, and the more rapidly the earthly planet will be spiritualized.

It is this higher spiritual presence that the author has felt very privileged to experience in memorable instances, when groups are led, in respect of the inherent laws of the seven life processes, to a deepening of the meaning of life experiences. Where one would normally expect to find the deepest experience of suffering (that is, in the stark acknowledgment of individual or corporate shortcomings or life challenges), the Easter experience of dying and becoming is made possible. Knowledge of the Christ is not a prerequisite for attaining this experience, nor is knowledge of any other spiritual level of existence. Nor is it necessary to know the seven life processes themselves. What

---

[125] Rudolf Steiner, *The Influence of Spiritual Beings upon Man*, June 1, 1908 lecture.

is absent in individual knowledge can be rebuilt through the wisdom present in the harmonious collaboration within a group. In *A Revolution of Hope*, I illustrated how that was the case in the collective process that culminated in Bill Wilson's coming to the inspiration of the twelve steps that are now famous. Here the seven life processes are at work, though little did AA's founder know about them. All of this is, one could remember, in accord with what Prokofieff has said about the first stages of the Path of Forgiveness, where spiritual knowledge is not necessary. Only in later stages does it become essential.

Karmic Research

Described above are practical applications on the path of Spirit Recollection, but not the whole extent of it. Karmic research plays as important a part, as Steiner illustrated in following the lives of individuals and their deeds across time. Conducting karmic research is a wholly different endeavor from natural-scientific research, which takes its departure from the Goethean mode of observation. Below we offer some examples taken from Steiner.

Karmic investigation offers great temptation to spin all sorts of illusory connections. There are indeed many sources of illusion. In looking at the life of an individual, little importance should be given to the person's external calling. It is actually rare that someone would reincarnate repeatedly within a given profession; that is, that a musician would reincarnate as a musician, or a scientist as a scientist. Destiny is little connected with such external elements. It is more concerned with soul forces, resistances of soul, and moral relationships. These can manifest and work out in a variety of callings. In the lecture of September 7, 1924, we find a good example of difficulties in conducting a spiritual investigation.[126] There Steiner offered the example of an unspecified man whose karma he was investigating. Nothing of the man's vocation allowed one to see into his past. However, he had a very peculiar habit. Every time he had to lecture, without exception, he would take out a handkerchief and blow his nose. This is a radical and extreme

---

[126] Steiner, *Karmic Relationships*, Volume 4.

example. Likewise, it was hard to find traces of Franz Schubert in his previous lives. What was important in that instance was his connection with his friend, Baron Von Spaun, for whom it was much easier to find the tracks.[127] Schubert was very poor, while Von Spaun, a true idealist, spent his life in the Treasury Offices in Austria, and later as a director of lotteries. Von Spaun took it upon himself to provide for many of the needs of Schubert. In a previous incarnation, Schubert, then a Moor, had cared for Von Spaun, a Prince of Castile who had to flee from his home and take refuge among his enemies.[128]

The example of Eugen Dühring is also very telling. He published works of physics and mathematics.[129] He also wrote a very self-complacent sort of autobiography (*Sache, Leben und Feinde*), and utterly malicious pamphlets such as *Die Überschätzung Lessings und dessen Anwaltschaft für die Juden* (*The Overestimation of Lessing and His Advocacy for the Jews*). He mixed personal material (often gossip) with scientific material, for example in his *History of Mechanics*. It took a long time for Steiner to find anything about Eugen Dühring. Steiner first used everything about Dühring that appealed to him the most. In so doing, Steiner met with countless incarnations, but those were just reflections of the present incarnation. Then an important detail came to the fore: at a certain age Dühring had turned totally blind. Steiner focused on that, and one incarnation came forward. During the eighth or ninth century, Dühring had been an iconoclast, and had fought for a cultural life devoid of images. However, later in life, he reinstated the use of images.

From this small review, it can be seen that karmic relationships can be investigated through close human relationships, engrained habits, physical characteristics or illnesses, among other things. But what is clear is that this is a completely different methodology from anything that has to do with the typical Goethean and phenomenological approach, which serves as a starting point in the natural sciences. Little has been done specifically in this field to follow what Steiner pioneered

---

[127] Steiner, *Karmic Relationships*, Volume 1, March 9, 1924 lecture.

[128] Steiner, *Karmic Relationships*, Volume 4, September 21, 1924 lecture.

[129] Steiner, *Karmic Relationships*, Volume 1, March 9, 1924 lecture.

with his karmic relationships lectures. An overview of what has been published is offered by T. H. Meyer in *Rudolf Steiner's Core Mission*, heading 31 of Chapter 4.

Seeing the roles cardinal individualities have played in successive incarnations offers a deeper understanding of history. Here is Spirit Recollection, not just for organizations and communities, but for the understanding of certain world spiritual impulses.

The author wants to point out that research has been done in this direction (though it is not primarily karmically oriented), in Prokofieff's monumental effort of Spirit Recollection in regard to the Anthroposophical Society in *May Human Beings Hear It*. That opus portrays the complex history of the Anthroposophical Society without sympathy or antipathy, simply showing the forces at work: both those forces that contributed to the Society's achievements, and those that led to the problems it faced at Steiner's death. This picture offers us the opportunity to understand our history anew by taking collective responsibility, rather than by pointing the finger at this or that important personality, group, or movement around Steiner, or after him. That we don't have much research in the field of karmic research is subordinate to the little work done at the practical level. In systematically reviewing the events of our lives we can start to unleash a perception for the forces of destiny, which will enable us to understand what forces are at work in the lives of others, or in the life of a community. Even Steiner, before entering the field of karmic research, had to awaken himself to a perception of the forces of destiny through the revelations of his own personal previous life as Aquinas.

Aristotelian or Platonist?

We may look at the whole of *Karmic Relationships*, Volumes 3 and 4, plus the Hague Conversation, as a tremendous effort at Spirit Recollection. Through these, Steiner was offering us a historical overview of what it means to be an anthroposophist; an understanding of this comes through our ability to see ourselves in the course of time, since we are now anthroposophists by virtue of having belonged to the hosts of Michael, and to the Michaelic Movement, in the course of time. It is therefore completely natural that Steiner asked us to move from a general understanding to a pointed and personal one. "Who are you?" he asks us with urgency. Are you a Platonist or an Aristotelian, an Old or a Young Soul? All of that is asked in order to awaken in us the activity of Spirit Recollection. And with the Last Address, Steiner moves into a cosmic preview of the future.

Steiner had various opportunities to highlight how important it is for each one of us to have a deeper sense of who we are, karmically speaking. And Steiner showed appreciation for all such efforts during his lifetime. Walter Johannes Stein and Eugen Kolisko discovered the relationship between Aristotle and Steiner on one hand, and Ita Wegman and Alexander the Great, on the other hand. Stein also perceived his own last incarnation, which was confirmed by Steiner. The same was true in even larger measure for D. N. Dunlop and Ludwig Polzer-Hoditz, who became able to understand their previous lives in depth. After Wilhelm Rath arrived at the karmic connection between Aquinas and Steiner while listening to a lecture, he wrote about it in an article for *Das Goetheanum*. On reading it, Steiner commented, "If more such articles were written in our Society, I would have no need to be ill."[130] Moreover, through Spirit Recollection, Steiner was hoping to balance out the tendency toward "anthroposophic intellectualism" in the Anthroposophical Society.

Concluding Remarks

In the way we have ordered the whole field of Spirit Recollection, a natural progression has emerged, which reflects both the stages of Prokofieff's Path of Forgiveness and of Steiner's exercises of Spirit Recollection. The field of practical applications covers the whole of experiential spirituality, including the highest levels of social technology. Here we are working with the first two stages of the Path of Forgiveness, leading first to tolerance and then to forgiveness. In terms of Steiner's exercise, we are moving up to the Lesser Karma Exercise, or taking responsibility for our own karma. This can be discerned in the Twelve Step program,

---

[130] Meyer, *Rudolf Steiner's Core Mission*, 153-54.

in Nonviolent Communication and in the whole of social technology at progressively larger organizational levels. And for these stages, as Prokofieff has discerned, it is not necessary to know spiritual science; only a desire to engage in practice is needed.

At a second stage, that of spiritual-scientific karmic research, beyond the practical applications, we move to "discovering the origin of the present in previous incarnations," which can be achieved either through the Moon-Sun-Saturn exercise, or the Greater Karma exercise. In Prokofieff's terms, these stages correspond to willingly taking on the karma of other human beings or karmic groups. There is no room in karmic investigation for mere curiosity. The one who researches into this field steps into a new karma. This part of the path can be walked only by those who have a working knowledge of anthroposophy.

We have reached the conclusion of an exploration in which it has appeared that Steiner conducted the tasks of not one, but two initiates on the world stage. To the author this reveals more fully what had remained a mesmerizing riddle. When one follows Steiner's life one sees many apparent detours that do not seem to form a continuity with prior tasks. Certainly, many events on the world stage explain why certain impulses had to be discontinued; such was the case for the onset of World War I. Still, many pursuits appeared to be dictated from outer circumstances, rather than deeper necessity. Such was the case for Steiner's work at the Workers University, or Steiner's need to pursue the matter of threefolding personally. This question must have presented itself to W. J. Stein who says in conclusion to his conversation with Steiner in 1922: "Two forces hold sway in his [Steiner's] life. On the one hand, there is all that he took on as his destiny by accepting Schröer's unsolved task as his own. On the other, there is everything that was included in his own destiny. Whoever reads the descriptions in his *Autobiography* with an awareness of this duality will frequently find references to it."

UNDERSTANDING OF THE SPIRIT AND CONSCIOUS EXPERIENCE OF DESTINY

(Letter to members # 17 of July 6, 1924)

This week something will be given in the communications addressed to members in these columns, which may serve to bring us to a further understanding of the weekly "Leading Thoughts."

The understanding of Anthroposophical truth can be furthered if the relation which exists between man and the world is constantly brought before the human soul.

When man turns his attention to the World into which he is born and out of which he dies, he is surrounded in the first place by the fullness of his sense-impressions. He forms thoughts about these sense-impressions.

In bringing the following to his consciousness: "I am forming thoughts about what my senses reveal to me as the world," he has already come to the point where he can contemplate himself. He can say to himself: In my thoughts "I" live. The world gives me the opportunity of experiencing *myself* in thought. I find myself in the thoughts in which I contemplate the world.

And continuing to reflect in this way, he ceases to be conscious of the world; he becomes conscious of the "I." He ceases to have the world before him; he begins to experience the self.

If the experience be reversed, and the attention directed to the inner life in which the world is mirrored, then those events emerge into consciousness which belong to our life's destiny, and in which our human self has flowed along from the point of time to which our memory goes back. In following up the events of his destiny, a man experiences his own existence.

In bringing this to his consciousness: "I with my own self have experienced something that destiny brought to me," a man has already come to the point where he will contemplate the world. He can say to himself: I was not alone in my fate; the world played a part in my experience. I willed this or that; the world streamed into my will. I find the world in my will when I experience this will in self-contemplation.

Continuing thus to enter into his own being, man ceases to be conscious of the self, he becomes conscious of the world; he ceases to experience himself, he becomes feelingly aware of the world.

I send my thoughts out into the world, there I find myself; I sink into myself, there I find the world. If a man experiences this strongly enough, he is confronted with the great riddles of the World and Man.

For to have the feeling: I have taken endless pains to understand the world through thinking, and after all there is but myself in this thinking—this gives rise to the first great riddle. And to feel that one's own self is formed through destiny, yet to perceive in this process the onward flow of world-happenings—this presents the second riddle.

In the experience of this problem of Man and the World germinates the frame of mind in which man can so confront anthroposophy that he receives from it in his inner being an impression which rouses his attention.

For anthroposophy asserts that there is a spiritual experience which does not lose the world when thinking. One can also live in thought. Anthroposophy tells of an inward experience in which one does not lose the sense-world when thinking, but gains the Spirit-world. Instead of penetrating into the ego in which the sense-world is felt to disappear, one penetrates into the Spirit-world in which the ego feels established.

Anthroposophy shows, further, that there is an experience of destiny in which one does not lose the self. In fate, too, one can still feel oneself to be active. Anthroposophy points out, in the impartial, unegoistic observation of human destiny, an experience in which one learns to love the world and not only one's own existence. Instead of staring into the world which carries the ego on the waves of fortune and misfortune, one finds the ego which shapes its own fate voluntarily. Instead of striking against the world, on which the ego is dashed to pieces, one penetrates into the self, which feels itself united with the course of events in the world.

Man's destiny comes to him from the world that is revealed to him by his senses. If then he finds his own activity in the working of his destiny, his real self rises up before him not only out of his inner being but out of the sense-world too.

If a person is able to feel, however faintly, how the spiritual part of the world appears in the self, and how the self proves to be working in the outer world of sense, he has already learned to understand anthroposophy correctly. For he will then realize that in anthroposophy it is possible to describe the Spirit-world, which the self can comprehend. And this will enable him to understand that in the sense-world the self can also be found—in a different way than by diving within. Anthroposophy finds the self by showing how the sense-world reveals to man not only sense-perceptions but also the after-effects of his life before birth and his former earthly lives.

Man can now gaze on the world perceptible to his senses and say: It contains not only color, sound, warmth; in it are active the experiences passed through by souls before their present earthly life. And he can look into himself and say: I find there not only my ego but, in addition, a spiritual world is revealed.

In an understanding of this kind, a person who really feels—who is not unmoved by—the great riddles of Man and the World, can meet on a common ground with the Initiate who in accordance with his insight is obliged to speak of the outer world of the senses as manifesting not only sensible perceptions but also the impressions of what human souls have done in their life before birth and in past earthly lives, and who has to say of the world of the inner self that it reveals spiritual events which produce impressions and are as effective as the perceptions of the sense-world.

The would-be active members should consciously make themselves mediators between what the questioning human soul feels as the problems of Man and the Universe, and what the knowledge of the Initiates has to recount, when it draws forth a past world out of the destiny of human beings, and when by strengthening the soul it opens up the perception of a spiritual world.

In this way, through the work of the would-be active members, the Anthroposophical Society may become a true preparatory school for the school of Initiates. It was the intention of the Christmas Assembly to indicate this very forcibly; and one who truly understands what that Assembly meant will continue to point this out until the sufficient understanding of it can bring the Society fresh tasks and possibilities again.

BIBLIOGRAPHY

Alcoholics Anonymous

- *Alcoholics Anonymous: The Story of How Many Thousands of Men and Women Have Recovered from Alcoholism,* (New York: Alcoholics Anonymous World Services, Third Edition, 1976),

- *Twelve Steps and Twelve Traditions* (New York: Alcoholics Anonymous, 1981).

Hiebel, Frederick, *The Gospel of Hellas: the Mission of Ancient Greece and the Advent of Christ* (New York: Anthroposophic Press, 1949).

Kirchner-Bockholt, Margaret and Erich, *Rudolf Steiner's Mission and Ita Wegman* (London: Rudolf Steiner Press, 1977)

Meyer, Thomas H.:

- *W.J. Stein/Rudolf Steiner, Dokumentation eines wegweisenden Zusammenwirkens,* edited by T. Meyer (Dornach: Philosophisch-Anthroposophischer Verlag, 1985).

- *Rudolf Steiner's Core Mission: the Birth and Development of Spiritual-Scientific Karma Research* (Forest Row, UK: Temple Lodge, 2010)

Pfeiffer, Ehrenfried, *On Rudolf Steiner's Mystery Dramas*, November 14, 1948 lecture (Spring Valley, NY: Mercury Press, 1988).

Prokofieff, Sergei O.:

- *The Occult Significance of Forgiveness* (London: Temple Lodge, 1991).

- *May Human Beings Hear It: The Mystery of the Christmas Conference* (London: Temple Lodge, 2004).

Rosenberg, Marshall B., *Nonviolent Communication: A Language of Compassion* (Encinitas, CA: Puddle Dancer Press, 1999).

Salman, Harry, *The Social World as Mystery Center: The Social Vision of Anthroposophy* (Seattle: Threefold Publishers, 1998).

Scharmer, Otto, *Theory U: Leading from the Emerging Future; The Social Technology of Presencing* (Cambridge, MA: Society for Organizational Learning, 2007).

Senge, Peter; Scharmer, C. Otto; Jaworski, Joseph and Flowers, Betty Sue, *Presence: Exploring Profound Change in People, Organizations and Society* (Cambridge, MA: Society for Organizational Learning, 2004).

Stanfield, R. Brian, *The Art of Focused Conversation: 100 Ways to Access Group Wisdom in the Workplace* (Gabriola Island, Canada: New Society Publishers, 2000).

Stein, Walter Johannes, *Rudolf Steiner's Life and Work,* (New York: St. George Publications, 1987).

Steiner, Rudolf:

- *Intuitive Thinking as a Spiritual Path: A Philosophy of Freedom*, 1894 (New York: Anthroposophic Press, 1995).

- *How to Know Higher Worlds: A Modern Path to Initiation*, 1904 (Hudson, NY: Anthroposophic Press, 1994).

- *From the History and Contents of the First Section of the Esoteric School, 1904-1914; Letters, Documents, and Lectures* (Great Barrington, MA: Steiner Books, 2010).

- *Freemasonry and Ritual Work, the Misraim Service: Letters, Documents, Ritual Texts, and Lectures from the History and Contents of the Cognitive-Ritual Section of the Esoteric School: 1904-14* (Great Barrington, MA: Steiner Books, 2007).

- *Brotherhood and the Struggle for Existence*, Rudolf Steiner, November 23, 1905 Lecture (Spring Valley, NY: Mercury Press, 1980).

- *Rosicrucian Wisdom, an Introduction*, 1907 (London: Rudolf Steiner Press, 2000).

- *The Stages of Higher Knowledge*, 1905-08, (Hudson, NY: Anthroposophic Press, 1967).

- Notes for Edouard Schuré in Barr, Alsace ("Barr Document"), September 1907, typescript.

- *The Influence of Spiritual Beings upon Man*, 1908 (Spring Valley, NY: Anthroposophic Press, 1982).

- *The East in the Light of the West*, 1909 (Blauvelt, NY: Garber Communications, 1986).

- *Three Lectures on the Mystery Dramas*, 1910 (Spring Valley, NY: Anthroposophic Press, 1983).

- *Four Mystery Dramas*, 1910-1913, (London: Rudolf Steiner Press, 1973)

- *Esoteric Christianity and the Mission of Christian Rosenkreutz*, 1911-12 (London: Rudolf Steiner Press, 2000).

- *Esoteric Lessons, 1904-1909: Lectures, Notes, Meditations, and Exercises by Rudolf Steiner* (London: Rudolf Steiner Press, 1987).

- *From Jesus to Christ*, 1911 (London: Rudolf Steiner Press, 1973).

- *Reincarnation and Karma*, 1912 (Hudson, NY: Anthroposophic Press, 1960).

- *Self-Education: Autobiographical Reflections: 1861-1893*, 1913 (Spring Valley, NY: Mercury Press, 1985).

- *Secrets of the Threshold*, 1913 (Hudson, NY: Anthroposophic Press, 1987).

- *Christ and the Human Soul*, 1914 (London: Rudolf Steiner Press, 1972).

- *Occult Reading, Occult Hearing*, 1914 (London: Rudolf Steiner Press, 1975).

- *Earthly Death and Cosmic Life*, 1918 (London: Rudolf Steiner Press, 1964).

- *The Challenge of the Times*, 1918 (Spring Valley, NY: Anthroposophic Press, 1941).

- *From Symptom to Reality in Modern History*, 1918 (London: Rudolf Steiner Press, 1976).

- *How Can Mankind Find the Christ*, 1919 (Hudson, NY: Anthroposophic Press, 1984).

- *Inner Aspect of the Social Question*, 1919 (London: Rudolf Steiner Press, 1974).

- *Mysteries of Light, of Space and of the Earth*, 1919 (New York: Anthroposophic Press, 1945)

- *The Cosmic New Year*, 1920 (London: Percy Lund, Humphries & Co. Ltd., 1932).

- *The Redemption of Thinking: A Study in the Philosophy of Thomas Aquinas*, 1920 (London: Hodder and Stoughton, 1956).

- *Spiritual Science as a Foundation for Social Forms*, 1920 (Hudson, NY: Anthroposophic Press, 1986).

- *Awakening to Community*, 1923 (Spring Valley, NY: Anthroposophic Press, 1974).

- *The Anthroposophic Movement*, 1923 (Bristol, UK: Rudolf Steiner Press, 1993).

- *Autobiography: Chapters in the Course of My Life: 1861-1907*, 1924 (Hudson, NY: Rudolf Steiner Press, 1999).

- *Rosicrucianism and Modern Initiation*, 1924 (London: Rudolf Steiner Press, 1982).

- *The Roots of Education*, 1924 (Hudson, NY: Anthroposophic Press, 1997).

- *Karmic Relationships*, Volumes 1 to 8, 1924 (London: Rudolf Steiner Press, 1977).

- *Anthroposophical Leading Thoughts: Anthroposophy as a Path of Knowledge; The Michael Mystery*, 1924 (London: Rudolf Steiner Press, 1998).

Tomberg, Valentin, *Group Work Articles*, 1930 and 1938 (Spring Valley, NY: Candeur Manuscripts, 1985).

Urieli, Baruch Luke, *Learning to Experience the Etheric World* (London: Temple Lodge, 1998).

van den Brink, Margreet, *More Precious Than Light: How Dialogue Can Transform Relationships and Build Community* (Stroud, UK: Hawthorn Press, 1996).

van Houten, Coenraad:

- *Awakening the Will: Principles and Processes in Adult Learning* (Forest Row, UK: Adult Education Network, 1995).

- *Practising Destiny* (London: Temple Lodge, 2000).

- *The Threefold Nature of Destiny Learning* (London: Temple Lodge, 2004).

von Manen, Hans Peter, *Twin Roads to the Millennium: The Christmas Conference and the Karma of the Anthroposophical Society*

Watts, Jean, *Guided Dialogue For Releasing Depth Wisdom*, at http://wikifoundryattachments.com/-3lwFFV7xW6uYeMw-Y9RMw72928

Wiesberger, Hella, *1879-1882: Années de Genèse de la Science Spirituelle Anthroposophique* (Genève, Switzerland: Editions Anthroposophiques Romandes, 1988).

Zeylmans, Emanuel, *Willem Zeylmans van Emmichoven: An Inspiration for Anthroposophy. A Biography.* (Forest Row, UK: Temple Lodge, 2002).

Zeylmans van Emmichoven, F. Willem, *The Foundation Stone*, (London: Rudolf Steiner Press, 1963).

Printed in the United States
By Bookmasters